Marketing Mind Prints

Also by Philip Kitchen

RAISING THE CORPORATE UMBRELLA

THE FUTURE OF MARKETING

THE RHETORIC AND REALITY OF MARKETING

Marketing Mind Prints

Edited by
Philip J. Kitchen

First published 2004 by
PALGRAVE MACMILLAN
Houndmills, Basingstoke, Hampshire RG21 6XS and
175 Fifth Avenue, New York, N. Y. 10010
Companies and representatives throughout the world

PALGRAVE MACMILLAN is the global academic imprint of the
Palgrave Macmillan division of St. Martin's Press, LLC and of
Palgrave Macmillan Ltd. Macmillan® is a registered trademark in
the United States, United Kingdom and other countries. Palgrave is
a registered trademark in the European Union and other countries.

ISBN 1–4039–0682–3 hardback

This book is printed on paper suitable for recycling and made
from fully managed and sustained forest sources.

A catalogue record for this book is available from the British Library.

Library of Congress Cataloging-in-Publication Data
Marketing mind prints / edited by Philip J. Kitchen.
     p. cm.
   Includes bibliographical references and index.
   ISBN 1–4039–0682–3 (cloth)
     1. Marketing. 2. Marketing–Management. 3. Interactive
marketing. 4. Relationship marketing. 5. Export marketing.
I. Kitchen, Philip J.

HF5415.M3153 2004
658.8–dc22   2003068748

10   9   8   7   6   5   4   3   2   1
13   12   11   10   09   08   07   06   05   04

Printed and bound in Great Britain by
Antony Rowe Ltd, Chippenham and Eastbourne

Contents

List of Tables

List of Figures

Notes on Contributors

Philip J. Kitchen, the Editor of this book, holds the Chair in Strategic Marketing at Hull University Business School, Hull University, UK. Prior to this he held the Martin Naughton Chair in Business Strategy, specialising in Marketing, at Queen's University, Belfast where he founded and directed the Executive MBA programme. At Hull, he teaches and carries out research in marketing management, marketing communications, corporate communications, promotion management, and international communications management and has a specific aim to build an active team of marketing researchers. Before Queen's he was Senior Lecturer in Marketing and Founder and Director of the Research Centre for Corporate and Marketing Communications within the Department of Marketing at Strathclyde University. A graduate of the CNAA (BA[Hons]) initially, he received Masters degrees in Marketing from UMIST (MSc) and Manchester Business School (MBSc) respectively, and his PhD from Keele University. Since 1984 he has been active in teaching and research in the communications domain. He is Founding Editor and now Editor-in-Chief of the *Journal of Marketing Communications* (Routledge Journals, 1995). He has published seven books so far, including:

- *Public Relations: Principles and Practice* (International Thomson, 1997)
- *Marketing Communications: Principles and Practice* (ibid, 1999)
- *Communicating Globally: An Integrated Marketing Approach* (2000), and
- *Raising the Corporate Umbrella: Corporate Communications in the 21st Century* (2001) – both with Don Schultz of Northwestern University (NTC Business Books, Chicago and Palgrave, London).
- *Marketing: The Informed Student Guide* (2001), with Tony Proctor (International Thomson).
- *The Future of Marketing: Critical 21st Century Perspectives* (2003), Palgrave-Macmillan: London; and
- *The Rhetoric and Reality of Marketing: An International Managerial Approach* (2003), Palgrave-Macmillan: London.

Dr. Kitchen has contributed to such journals as the Journal of Advertising Research, Journal of Business Ethics, International Journal of

Market Research, International Journal of Advertising, Journal of Marketing Management, European Journal of Marketing, Marketing Intelligence and Planning, Journal of Marketing Communications, ADMAP, Journal of Nonprofit and Public Sector Marketing, International Journal of Bank Marketing, Journal of Corporate Communications, Small Business and Enterprise Development, Creativity and Innovation Management; and, numerous practitioner journals. Dr. Kitchen founded, organised, and chaired the 1st International Conference on Marketing and Corporate Communications and was Editor of the Proceedings (Keele, 1996, Strathclyde, 1998). This Conference is now an annual event (Antwerp, Belgium, 1997; Glasgow, Scotland, 1998; Salford, England, 1999; Erasmus Universiteit, The Netherlands, 2000; Queen's, 2001; Antwerp, 2002). Dr. Kitchen serves on the Editorial Advisory Board of the Journal of Marketing Management and is a Review Board Member of Marketing Intelligence and Planning and Corporate Communications: An International Journal. He is an Adjunct Professor at Massey University, New Zealand.

He has given papers on marketing management, corporate or marketing communications in England, Scotland, Czech Republic, Estonia, France, Germany, Belgium, Portugal, Australia, New Zealand, Spain, The Republic of Ireland, Northern Ireland, Israel, The Netherlands, and in the United States.

He is also active in the professional arena. He is a member of the Measurement Academic Advisory Panel (MAAP) with Hill Knowlton, Inc which involves leading academics from Europe, Pacific Rim, and America. This group seeks to bring a robust academic dimension to H&K thinking across a wide range of measurement evaluation tools.

Malcolm H.B. McDonald (Emeritus Professor) MA (Oxon), MSc, PhD, D.Litt. FCIM FRSA, was, until recently, Professor of Marketing and Deputy Director Cranfield School of Management with special responsibility for E-Business, is a graduate in English Language and Literature from Oxford University, in Business Studies from Bradford University Management Centre, and has a PhD from Cranfield University. He also has an honorary Doctorate from Bradford University. He has extensive industrial experience, including a number of years as Marketing Director of Canada Dry.

He is Chairman of six companies and spends much of his time working with the operating boards of the world's biggest multinational companies, such as IBM, Xerox, BP and the like, in most countries in the world, including Japan, USA, Europe, South America, ASEAN and Australasia.

He has written 38 books, including the best seller 'Marketing Plans; how to prepare them; how to use them' and many of his papers have been published.

His current interests centre on the use of information technology in advanced marketing processes.

Dale Littler is Professor of Marketing at the Manchester School of Management and Dean of Management Studies at UMIST. He graduated with a first class honours degree from the University of Manchester, where he also obtained his doctorate. He joined the Manchester Business School where he was engaged in research aimed at examining various facets of the economic and social effects of technological innovation. Following a brief spell at Liverpool University Business School, he moved to UMIST.

He has received research grants from the ESRC, CIMA, and various commercial organisations. He was a Principal Investigator on the ESRC funded programme on Information and Communication Technologies, and has been involved in several Teaching Company Schemes (TCS) of which the scheme for Xpert Systems won the 2002 ESRC award for the best application of Management or Social Science.

He has written several books, and published extensively in marketing and technology journals. He has been a member of the ESRC Research Grants Board. He is currently a Member of the Academic Senate of the Chartered Institute of Marketing (CIM), Chair of the Academy of Marketing Research Committee, and Chair of the CIM–Academy of Marketing Research Forum Working Party.

Jacob Goldenburg is Senior Lecturer at the Hebrew University of Jerusalem, School of Business Administration. He received a joint PhD degree on inventive thinking from this school and the Racach Institute of Physics at the Hebrew University. His bachelors degree was in aeronautical engineering, and his masters degree in mechanical engineering.

He has taught modules and workshops in inventive thinking for many high-technology companies and marketing organisations in both Israel and the USA, and has worked with companies such as Scitex, Intel, Motorola, MasterCard, Ogilvy & Mather, and Rapp & Collins.

Dr. Goldenburg has published papers in leading journals such as Science, Journal of Marketing, Journal of Marketing Research, Management Science, Marketing Science, and the Harvard Business Review. He is co-author of *Creativity in Product Innovation*.

He is shortly to take up a Visiting Professorial post at Columbia University.

Stanley J. Paliwoda has been Professor of International Marketing at the Birmingham Business School, University of Birmingham since 1999 and was previously Professor and Chair at the University of Calgary, Canada. He is the author or co-author of fifteen books including International Marketing, now being prepared in its 4th edition. His books have been translated into foreign languages including Chinese and Spanish.

He was elected a Fellow of the Chartered Institute of Marketing in 1993, a Fellow of the Chartered Management Institute in 2002, and has just been appointed Chair of the Professional Education and Qualification Board of the Institute of Export. He is listed in a number of international directories including *Who's Who in the World*.

John K. Ryans Jnr holds the James R. Good Chair in Global Strategy at Bowling Green State University. Formerly, he was Bridgestone Chair in International Business and Marketing at Kent State University. A DBA graduate of Indiana University, Dr. Ryans is one of the 50 members of the Fellows of the Academy of International Business, a 3,000 member organisation, and a member of the American Marketing Association Foundation's Leadership Council. The author or co-author of 20+ books and 100+ articles in major journals, he has been a consultant to many leading US and foreign firms, including Novo Industri, McCann Erickson, Goodyear International, Xerox and the US departments of Commerce and Education, and he has designed and/or presented in-house training programs for many firms, including Digital Equipment, Firestone and Nestle.

Angus Jenkinson has over 15 years experience as a leader in the field of customer relationship management, working with major international organisations such as OgilvyOne, Vodafone, IBM, Thomson Tours Group, The National Trust and WWF International to help them enhance customer loyalty and organisational strategy, technology and practice. He is the author of *Valuing Your Customers* and chairman of Stepping Stones Consultancy Ltd, a highly respected organisation and customer development consultancy firm in the UK. In addition to his consulting projects, he is a regular keynote speaker at major conferences on this theme, as well as having presented scores of workshops to managers internationally. He has recently taken up the chair of integrated at a UK business school to lead research into major CRM issues.

Branko Sain is a Research Fellow at the CFIM and an Associate of the Stepping Stones Consultancy. He started his career as a Marketing Executive for a large sports organisation. Over the last few years he has undertaken academic research projects for masters and doctoral programs, and a number of consultancy assignments for both commercial and non-profit organisations. He has been involved in leading academic programs, supervising research projects and teaching marketing modules at university level. He has conducted research and published works for both practitioner and academic audiences.

Charles Chien is Associate Professor of Marketing at, and Director of the Department of International Trade and Business, Feng Chia University, Taiwan. He was a Visiting Scholar at the Department of Business and Management, University of Glasgow, Scotland UK. He holds a PhD in Marketing from University of Wales, UK. His main academic interests are in relationship marketing, customer relationship management, and cross cultural management. He has carried out extensive consultancy regarding Taiwanese firms' marketing strategy in mainland China.

Luiz Moutinho is Foundation Chair in Marketing at Glasgow University Management School in Glasgow, Scotland, UK. His main teaching interests include: quantitative analysis in marketing management, research methods, strategic marketing and Futurecast, consumer behaviour, marketing of services (tourism & banking), and environmental scanning & strategy. His research interests are focused upon: computer modelling in marketing management, consumer behaviour and statistical model building, tourism marketing, and bank marketing. He has published several books, and many papers on these topics in national and international media. He is a review board member for many marketing journals.

Acknowledgements

With grateful thanks to the outstanding group of contributors, for sharing their knowledge, expertise, understanding, and experience, with readers of this book. Their expertise and cooperation has been invaluable.

I acknowledge, with the contributors, the various individuals, companies, and research journals who have assisted us by allowing material to be cited and shared. Also, we thank the many myriads of marketing students who through their questions and comments have helped the authors sharpen and hone their critical faculties. And we must also acknowledge the literally thousands of practitioners and colleagues who through workshops, seminars, conferences, and symposia have influenced development of the thoughts expressed in this book.

To all of you, thank you for your help, guidance, support, and encouragement, to be able to offer critical perspectives on the discipline of marketing, what it is, and what it may yet become, as we move forward in the 21st century.

Philip J. Kitchen
The Editor

1
Introduction to Marketing Mind Prints

Philip J. Kitchen

This edited book is the final part of a trilogy commencing with *The Future of Marketing* (2003), and *The Rhetoric and Reality of Marketing* (2003) published by Palgrave-Macmillan. In the first book, leading theorists such as Jagdish Sheth, Stephen Brown, Walter van Waterschoot, Els Gilbrecht and others developed their own critical perspectives on marketing and what the future might hold for the discipline. It seems evident that alternative forms of marketing have been developed, are currently under development, or will be developed in the future. Put another way, the received wisdom associated with the managerial school of marketing is under question. Beyond that, many other questions are being raised about the value of marketing and particularly in terms of its bottom-line contribution. Yet, simultaneously, the move from conquest to curriculum marketing, means that marketing is more important today then ever before, but not necessarily in the same form as that proposed in leading marketing texts. Certainly, any radical change in the marketing concept or in marketing practice cannot be implemented rapidly.

In the second book, marketing in eight nation states were explored by means of two case studies – one in which firms practiced marketing as a form of rhetoric, the other where marketing and its insights were driven deeply into the organisational psyche. A reasoned, yet simultaneous jaundiced, conclusion, was that for many organisations, marketing is no more and no less than a form of window dressing, or gloss, while the real focus of marketing attention – i.e. living, breathing customers and consumers are given – at best – lip service. It is this type of marketing – without form or substance, save in the word itself, that is giving the discipline with all of its diverse heritage, a bad name.

These first two books in the trilogy discussed marketing in terms of its contribution to business and society. Both were attempts to help explain marketing in terms different to those found in leading texts. Marketing is indeed a powerful business discipline, it does help create (apparently) satisfactory exchanges – certainly they are satisfactory to the many companies practicing the concept. However, there is still a sense of profound unease concerning marketing as a discipline. For, to any student of marketing, particularly in the United Kingdom, a mere walk to the local shopping centre, or attempting to communicate with a utility company, or gain access to inexpensive and worthwhile public transport, is hedged around with ambivalence, discourtesy, sheer bad management, and a perception that customer needs come pretty close to last on any organisational agenda. That is why, in the previous books I referred to 'the jaundiced model of marketing'. It is one thing to talk of a business philosophy and practice that is aimed toward satisfying consumer needs. Then, to couple this philosophy with a range of concepts and tools (mostly borrowed from other academic disciplines), that ostensibly deliver customer and organisational satisfactions. And, to openly proclaim the philosophy or concept in educational foras. It is quite another thing to see many business, apparently enjoying continued profitable lives, which patently make no attempt whatsoever to cater for customer needs in any way, apart from the obvious one of payment for goods provided or services rendered. It is also disconcerting to see many non-profit and public sector organisations adopting the trappings of marketing (i.e. advertising, public relations, and other promotional tools) and proclaiming in whatever way – customer orientation, and yet simultaneously plainly displaying sales or production orientation. In a society where more and more public sector organisations are forced into market posturing, rather than adopt and rigorously integrate marketing as a reality, they settle for the watered-down milksop version evidently considered appropriate by political task masters.

Background

This third part of the trilogy draws upon the views, comments, criticisms, and opinions of leading marketing theorists around the world. There is, however, no overt attempt here to constrain the contributors to particular topics. By 'marketing mind prints', this book is not attempting to 'map' the future by indicating the nature of the terrain and the ways to traverse it. Instead, contributors are asked to develop a 'mind print', that is a picture of a segment of the marketing terrain that they consider to be important now and in the future. The aim is for readers to ponder on a specific mind print, and to consider how and in what ways the print can be incorporated or developed within their own specific business.

The essay is chosen as the medium of presentation deliberately. As writers, we are more used to articles, usually developed using the scientific approach, as might be found, for example, in the *Journal of Marketing, Harvard Business Review* and the like. Here, there is no attempt to eschew the scientific method or form. Instead, an essay can be more personal, even anecdotal, often using first person narrative.

An executive management text

The book itself is conceived as suitable for executives. That is, it is targeted to senior managers who are charged with and challenged by the need to re-think, revise and revitalize the marketing activities of their companies and who may travel frequently across the country and around the world. The text is deliberately short, provocative and personalised, and draws on numerous examples. It is anticipated that the book can easily be dipped into, perhaps read within a few short hours. However, during those hours, a print of some element of what marketing is, or is in process of becoming, can be left in the mind. Thus, the content is focussed on self-discovery and illumination, and not on direction.

Our market

More than likely readers are:

- Senior practitioners in marketing, marketing management, and related disciplines such as marketing communication, market research, public relations, advertising, sales and their like, primarily those in national, international, trans-national, multi-national, and global organisations.
- Members of professional institutes such as the Chartered Institute of Marketing (CIM) in the UK, the American Marketing Association (AMA) and Promotion Marketing Association (PMA) in the US, and other similar groups around the world.
- Graduate students studying for an MBA in Marketing or courses in which marketing plays a prominent role, either as a stream of study, or as a specialist option.

- Those interested in the concept and philosophy of marketing, as a business and societal force focussed upon improved organisational performance and delivering customer satisfactions more effectively and efficiently than competitors.

Marketing mind prints

In this book, we explore seven mind prints:

- Marketing mind prints (Philip Kitchen)
- Marketing due diligence and the future of marketing (Malcolm McDonald)
- Innovation and sustainable competitive advantage (Dale Littler)
- Invisible forces: how consumer interactions make the difference (Jacob Goldenberg)
- Landmarks in the mapping of international marketing (Stan Paliwoda and John K. Ryans Jnr)
- Integrated marketing: a new vision (Angus Jenkinson and Branko Sain)
- Beyond relationship marketing (Charles Chien and Luiz Moutinho)

Obviously, we not expect the book to be read as a continuous narrative. A hackneyed expression may be for readers to 'pick and mix'. Read the essays that interest and concern you and your business. Pick up and put down. Authors are a little like boiled sweets – some are easy to digest, others less so. It is up to you. Nonetheless, there are strands, connections, and interrelations among all the essays. To paraphrase Virginia Wolf – marketing is not like a series of landing gear lights symmetrically arranged, it is instead a series of lights inside marketers minds, switched on by market need, translated into behaviours (i.e. products, services, prices, communications, and distribution) that persuade consumers and customers to buy, and continually refreshed in the workshop of thought and practice. Marketing myopia reduces the lights to a dull and continuous dim glow, with an expectation that the same fish will always be there in an unchanging sea of repetitive behaviours.

Marketing mind prints

I firstly describe what I mean by marketing mind prints. The idea of a mind print is not new, in fact is seems to be an ancestral fossil genetically printed into the minds and behaviours of every human being. I believe, after some delving into various strands of literature, that this is the first time the mind print concept has been applied to marketing.

Marketing due diligence and the future of marketing

Malcolm McDonald, in his usual forthright and erudite manner, then tackles the topic of marketing due diligence and the future of marketing. The real question, and I dare say, the telling issue for every company, is how marketing contributes to shareholder value, and how that contribution can be measured. He is obviously not alone in this quest, as marketing is now under the microscope of managerial and executive attention. Quite rightly, as one of the leading thinkers on marketing in the UK, he questions where the future of marketing lies.

Innovation and sustainable competitive advantage

For the past two decades, Dale Littler of UMIST, has been exploring innovation and its contribution to sustainable competitive advantage. Businesses that do not innovate will be left behind in the swirling tides of competitive forces. Managers that do not innovate will continue to manage (doubtless) in the time honoured manner described in *The Peter Principle*. Failure to innovate means failure to sustain current competitive advantage, and further rusts the locked door leading to future developments. Hardly advantageous!

Invisible forces: how consumer interactions make the difference

Why do new products fail? Why do marketing communications programmes fail? Are there, in fact, invisible forces which influence success or failure? Jacob Goldenberg of the Hebrew University of Jerusalem and Columbia University, shows that they can and do. Revisiting an old, yet ever vital, theme, the failure of products and programmes may actually be a failure of managers and executives to think and manage creatively. His mind print indicates how and in what ways ideation and creativity can be honed by scientific tools and professional training. Jacobs' recent series of articles in the *Journal of Marketing*, *Harvard Business Review* and the like, are indicative of the need for such training.

Landmarks in the mapping of international marketing

I like the idea of landmarks in a book concerning 'mindprints'. Here, Stan Paliwoda and John K. Ryans illustrate and illuminate several current landmarks in the international marketing landscape. International marketing has to become part of every marketers' mindscape – as products and services are not limited by geographic factors, but are limited by managerial ability to conceive and tackle market opportunities. Unlike most marketers, Stan and John, predict international developments. Check your activities against their checklist! They also present eight continuing and future challenges for marketers.

Integrated marketing: a new vision

Few readers in the marketing world will not have heard the word 'integration'. Indeed, it is a word or activity that has taxed my mind over recent years. Here, Angus Jenkinson and Branko Sain discuss the new vision that is styled 'integrated marketing'. What is 'integrated marketing'? How does it work? How does it differ from previous old-fashioned un-integrated marketing? The answers, or at least some answers are here. Drawing directly on a range of recent studies (case and empirical) with leading blue-chip and other companies, Angus and Branko present not one, but 18 key elements which can be applied by any company – the vision operationalised.

Beyond relationship marketing

This is the final mind print, and perhaps not one for the faint-hearted or marketing beginner. Charles Chien and Luiz Moutinho intend to provoke mental stretching and stimulation by their discussion of relationship marketing – and they succeed! They go beyond the known, the tried, and the tested. Some new mind print ideas include presentation and non-presentation (no, these are not spelling mistakes), reciprocal dispersion, personification, and provide many definitions of elements under the banner of relationship marketing: utility, exchange utility, projectability, exchange solidarity (internal and external), reciprocity, legitimacy, relationship exchange, and finally – relationship marketing itself. Ideas discussed here may have resonance for many private and public sector organisations.

I would be interested in hearing from readers concerning other important 'marketing mind prints'. I'd be very interested in viewing marketing from a consumer or consumption perspective.

2
Marketing Mind Prints
Philip J. Kitchen

My own views on marketing are recorded in the two previous books in this edited trilogy. Ideas in marketing come from many diverse disciplines. In writing this book, my mind went back at least twenty years, to a book read as an undergraduate (non-marketing) student. Virginia Woolf (1984) in an essay titled *Modern Fiction* wrote:

> Examine for a moment an ordinary mind on an ordinary day. The mind receives a myriad impressions – trivial, fantastic, evanescent, or engraved with the sharpness of steel. From all sides they come, an incessant shower of innumerable atoms; and as they fall, as they shape themselves into the life of Monday or Tuesday, the accent falls differently from of old; the moment of importance came not here but there …

> Life is not a series of gig lamps symmetrically arranged; life is a luminous halo, a semi-transparent envelope surrounding us from the beginning of consciousness to the end.   (pp. 149–50)

Now, it is worth asking the question: In what way is the mind of a marketer different than other minds? (no facetious or fatuous comments here, please). Surely his/her mind also receives myriad impressions? And true, they will indeed shape themselves into Monday, or Thursday and so forth. Yet, underlying these impressions is [presumably] the teaching, doctrine, philosophy, practice or essence of something known as 'marketing' or 'the marketing concept'. And that concept, has to be applied in specific contextual circumstances – in, for example, a consumer, industrial, business-to-business, not for profit, or public sector context. Moreover, entailed within marketing is the necessity to strategise, plan, operationalise, evaluate, and of course, fit in the usual daily routine. The difficult part in this is that it can all be seen from inside-out. What many marketers need to do is adopt an outside-in perspective – i.e. the product, price, delivery, advertising and so forth, as interpreted in the minds of receivers or customers. That is far more difficult, but still has to be incorporated into daily decisions made, and preferably – 'engraved with the sharpness of steel'.

Now, we can pursue the second paragraph. Marketing cannot be viewed as a set of commandments hewn in tablets of stone and brought down from Mount Kotler or whoever or whatever else happens to be the leading doyen (or among the leaders) of its exposition. Instead, inside the mind of an average marketer, there will be no gig lamps of principles symmetrically laid down, instead we may find something resembling Woolf's luminous (or not so luminous) halo surrounding us from the beginning of our marketing career to the end. It is the task of this and other books in the trilogy to attempt to convey this varying and variable spirit. Some of it may well seem alien and external, but perhaps in 2104, maybe marketing itself will be seen in this light. In the minds of readers we find the ideas and ideals of customer service, consumer orientation, competitive intelligence, return on investment, sales, profits, market share, and all the rest. We assume that these mind prints are derived from: marketing training (likely in the dominant managerial school); marketing practice – perhaps having ascended through the school of hard knocks in terms of sales; personal reading or self-instruction. For most marketers, it will be a combination of all three. The unfortunate intuitive 'I know what's best' seat-polishing marketer is not part of this group, even though intuition may last for a goodly while.

For the rest, the not so intuitive, we are concerned to discover how mind prints are developed, and, of course, later in the book, we illustrate some new, or old, or redirections in this regard.

There is no escape from one's own mind prints. They can only be augmented and developed, never extinguished, save by neglect. I am reminded of Calvino's immortal lament of a learned professor:

> The professor is there at his desk; in the cone of light from a desk lamp his hands surface, suspended, or barely resting on the closed volume, as if in a sad caress …
>
> 'Reading,' he says, 'is always there: there is a thing that is there, a thing made of writing, a solid material object, which cannot be changed, and through this thing we measure ourselves against

something else that is not present, something else that belongs to the ... world, because [now] it can only be thought, imagined, or because it once was and is no longer, past, lost, unattainable, in the land of the dead'.   (*Source*: Calvino 1981)

Thus, mindprints belong in minds, and the ones provided in this book, if pondered upon and applied will make their way via exposure, attention, comprehension, acceptance, yielding (persuasion), to retention in the long term memory, to be used as guideposts in planning and implementing marketing for the purpose of exchange. Through reading, we measure the theory and ourselves against more cogent realities – out there in the hurly-burly world of tinkling cash registers, of exchange, of competitive forces, of markets. Unless we fail to apply the lessons, today, like Calvino's lament, our travels and travails will be to no avail.

In preparing this chapter, I was unaware initially that the concept of a mind print or mindprints was in fact well known and considered in many diverse fields of intellectual activity, albeit *not* marketing. A brief check via google.com search on mind prints was enough to disabuse me of this wrong thinking. I was particularly impressed by a paper by Tsion Avital titled 'MindPrints: The Structural Shadows of Mind Reality'. Avital states:

> In a minimal sense, mindprints are fundamental properties or attributes of human intelligence, *or the interfaces between mind and reality*. In a broader sense, it appears that mindprints are common to all levels of Being, and are therefore epistemological and ontological oxymorons, or metastructures of the complementarity of mind and reality. *In other words, mindprints are the bridge between epistemology and ontology*. (italics added here, see p. 3 of Avital's paper).

Although I am working in an entirely different field than Avital, there is a similar recognisance that a mindprint – perhaps derived from some of the sources alluded to earlier – connects what goes on in the mind with what happens in the real world of exchange. For example, a cursory study of marketing to many students may indicate that it is all *just common sense*. The concept and tools of marketing are, in fact, simple and easy to understand. But their application is evidently not so simple or easy to understand. For apparently, many businesses and their staff seem incapable in terms of application. Even marketing students devoid of intellectual curiosity, and there are many of these too, must observe a huge abyss yawning between what is taught in the lecture theatre and seminar room, and what is actually practiced out there in the marketplace. It may be that part of marketing's failures, is traceable to a weak idea of the simplicity of marketing. Yet, fundamentally, marketing is not simple. It takes real work to understand, real effort to apply, costs huge sums to get it right, and many thousands – perhaps millions of man hours – to drive the concept deeply into an organisational psyche. Even then, it needs to be refreshed by the exigencies of competitive, consumer and other forms of marketing reality, for what worked yesterday, will not work tomorrow. Perhaps poor marketing may be no more and no less, than a poorly understood mindprint in marketers as to what marketing actually is. If experimentation were to take place, it may be found that mindprints of marketing staff in 'successful' businesses will be radically different than those in lesser organisations.

Let me now explore the two constructs of epistemology and ontology. I can see managers backing away here, but stay with me for a while.

Marketing epistemology

This concerns the nature, sources, and limits of knowledge in the marketing discipline. One problem with 'marketing' perse is that none of its propositions can be described as true and applicable at all times and places. For example, what passed as marketing in Henry Ford's day of Model T's, would be laughably absurd in our day, as Kwik Save found to its cost. Likewise, marketing's late focus on customers as kings, and now shareholders as kings, would cut little ice perhaps one hundred years from now. Thus knowledge in and of marketing presupposes that the mind of the individual is set in some particular culture and time-constrained setting. For example, my own epistemological views on marketing are described in Chapter 1 of *The Future of Marketing*. They are dependent for their validity (to me) on the epistemological odyssey undertaken, an odyssey that is presumably different for every marketer (academic or practitioner) (see Kitchen 2003a), while still allowing for commonalities in terms of shared epistemology.

Many marketers would – correctly in my view – claim that their own basic beliefs concerning marketing are based on actual marketing experience, their own innate skills, or that what they do may be seen as the norm in given cultural circumstances. Philosophically, few can argue against these positions. Also, some marketers may argue that their views are based on sound underlying principles from related disciplines (i.e. economics and psychology for exa… would argue here either.

The point I am driving at, is that marketers ne… own current epistemology. What do they know, they know this? What are the sources of the know… knowledge they have being advanced, upgraded, or d… few well-learned perhaps early lessons, plus adult… suffice? One perhaps related theme of the book is to … a light on current mindprints in order to develop still further, or even better to displace outworn outmoded mindprints with newer more relevant ones.

The fact is that most marketers will struggle to keep pace with what is happening in their marketing domain. The shifting sands of market need and share, sales, competitive forces, data gathering and analysis, and of the myriad tools required to measure, monitor, influence, and attempt to persuade and retain customers and consumers, all form part of mindprints. Beyond that, the need to perform, progress, develop and accentuate a career presumably have some relevance. The marketer, in order to progress, has to explore these facets continuously. For, if we keep on doing what we do now, it will certainly lead to failure, as market forces change around us.

Marketing ontology

The word 'ontology' refers to the philosophical investigation of existence or being. Such investigation may be directed towards the concept of being asking 'what being means, or what it is for something to exist; it may also or instead be concerned with deeper question: what exists. It is common to speak of a [marketing] philosopher's ontology, meaning the kind of things they take to exist, or the ontology of a theory, meaning the things that would have to exist for the theory to be true. (*Source*: Routledge Encyclopedia of Philosophy)

Again, my own view concerning ontology from a marketing perspective has been previously stated in the 'castle metaphor' (see Kitchen 2003b). Here, we are interested in a marketers ontology, and particularly seeking to compare what actually exists with what is known. Ontologically, marketers as in any other discipline occasionally means asking the question: what is it I do? Or, why is this significant? Or, is it important that this be done? Perhaps, even, what is my contribution in terms of success and failure? Am I making a contribution? How can this be honed, sharpened or further developed?

perjorative sense, marketing epistemology and ontology are not
moronic, for these terms are not incongruous or contradictory.
What is oxymoronic is the holding of certain mind prints (say the
tenets of managerial marketing for example) in the mind of marketers
which bear no resemblance to the reality encountered by customers
and consumers in a given marketplace.

For example, in an earlier book, I said ... 'the application of marketing – *ostensibly in the name of customers and consumers* – of benefits
(utilities) they may receive, *is often no more than a rhetorical device*.
In business after business, and industry after industry, apparent ...
innovations are introduced which annoy, confuse, and irritate customers. They are in fact no more than organisational innovations
designed to create organisational inefficiencies by keeping customers –
the life blood of the organisation – at a distance. Very few organisations are really interested in the customers whose needs they claim to
serve' (Kitchen 2003b, italics added). Thus, on the one hand we have
businesses (or their managers) claiming to be adopting and using the
marketing concept on behalf (a form of knowledge or epistemology).
Yet, on the other hand, what companies actually do in the marketplace
is, in some way, fundamentally flawed. Thus, ontologically, something
in terms of marketing reality has to exist, and this 'something' has to
deliver what is apparently promised. It is in this apparent discontinuity
between epistemology and ontology, that is oxymoronic. Therefore, a
mind print or mindprints has to become the bridge over which marketers pass in improving their own knowledge and, concomitantly, the
experiences customers and consumers receive.

With these few words, I will now let readers pass on over the various
bridges or mindprints provided by contributors to this book.

Let me reiterate a point made elsewhere. I would welcome views,
opinions, and comments concerning other mindprints which are not
stated here.

References

Avital, T. (2003) 'MindPrints: The Structural Shadows of Mind Reality' due to
appear in a special edition of *Symmetry; Culture, and Literacy*, see also:
avital_t@netvision.net.il
Calvino, I. (1981) 'If on a Winter's Night a Traveller'. Tr. William Weaver.
Harcourt Brace: New York.
Kitchen, P.J. (2003a) Editor *The Future of Marketing: Critical 21st Century
Perspectives*, Palgrave-Macmillan, Basingstoke; pp. 3–11; 173–179.
Kitchen, P.J. (2003b) Editor *The Rhetoric and Reality of Marketing: An International
Managerial Approach*, Palgrave-Macmillan, Basingstoke; pp. 8–11.

Routledge Encyclopedia of Philosophy edited by Craig, E. (1998), see: http:www.rep.routledge.com, London: Routledge.
Woolf, V. (1984) Essay titled 'Modern Fiction' quoted in full in *The Common Reader: First Series*, Ed. McNeillie, A. Harcourt Brace Jovanovich/First Harvest.

3
Marketing Due Diligence and the Future of Marketing

Malcolm McDonald

Introduction

The ultimate test of marketing investment, and indeed any investment, is whether it creates value for shareholders. But, few marketing investments are evaluated from this perspective, and many would argue that it is almost impossible to link financial results to any specific marketing activity (Shaw R. et al. 2002).

Increasingly, boards of directors and city analysts the world over are dissatisfied with this lack of accountability for what are, very often, huge budgets. Cranfield School of Management has been addressing this problem through its Marketing Value Added Research Club, formed with a number of blue-chip companies. The club sets out to create and test a new framework which shows how marketing systematically contributes to shareholder value, and how its contribution can be measured in an objective and comparable way.

There is an urgent need for such a framework. Not only does marketing need it to answer the widespread accusations of poor performance, but corporate and financial strategists need it too, to understand how to link marketing activities to the wider corporate agenda. All too often marketing objectives and strategies are not aligned with the organisation's overall plans to increase shareholder value.

The purpose of this essay is to set out the logic of this framework, which is underpinned by a prize-winning Cranfield PhD (Wilson H. 1996).

The essay starts with a brief justification of the need for a wholly new approach to measuring the effectiveness of marketing.

What counts as marketing expenditure?

Historically, marketing expenditure has tended to escape rigorous performance appraisal for a number of reasons. Firstly, there has been real confusion as to the true scope and nature of marketing investments. Too often, marketing expenditure has been assumed to be only the budgets put together by the marketing function, and as such, a (major) cost to be controlled rather than a potential driver of value. Secondly, the causal relationship between expenditure and results has been regarded as too difficult to pin down to any useful level of precision (Shaw R. et al. 2002).

Now, because of the demands of increasingly discerning customers and greater competition, marketing investments and marketing processes are under scrutiny as never before (Denison and McDonald 1995, Shaw and Mazur 1997, Clark 1999, Piercy 1999, Doyle 2000). From the process point of view, as a result of insights from management concepts such as the quality movement and re-engineering, marketing is now much more commonly seen as a cross-functional responsibility of the entire organisation rather than just the marketing department's problem (Denison and McDonald 1995, Doyle 1998, Piercy 1999).

Howard Morganis, past Chairman of Proctor and Gamble said,

> There is no such thing as a marketing skill by itself. For a company to be good at marketing, it must be good at everything else from R&D to manufacturing, from quality controls to financial controls.   (Davidson H. 1997)

In relation to this statement, Davidson (1997) comments:

> Marketing is an approach to business rather than a specialist discipline. It is no more the exclusive responsibility of the marketing department than profitability is the sole charge of the finance department.

There is therefore a growing awareness that, because of this wider interpretation of marketing, nearly all budgets within the company could be regarded as marketing investments in one way or another (Ward 1989, Walters and Halliday 1997, Shaw 1998). This is especially the case with IT budgets. The exponential increase in computing power has made it possible to track customer perceptions and behaviours on a far greater scale, and with far greater precision than previously. When used correctly, these databases and analytical tools can shed a much greater light on what really happens inside the 'black box'. However, the sums involved in acquiring such technologies are forcing even the most slapdash of companies to apply more rigorous appraisal techniques to their investments in this area (Stone et al. 2000).

This wider understanding of what 'marketing' is really all about has had a number of consequences. Firstly, the classic textbook treatment of strategic issues in marketing has finally caught up with reality. Topics such as market and customer segmentation, product and brand development, databases and customer service and support are now regularly discussed at board level, instead of being left to operational managers or obscure research specialists.

CEOs and MDs are increasingly accepting that they must take on the role of chief marketing officer if they want to create truly customer-led organisations. Sir Clive Thompson of Rentokil commented:

> I am convinced that corporate and marketing strategy are more or less the same things. The chief executive has to be the chief marketer. If you delegate that responsibility, you are not doing your job.   (Shaw 1998)

Secondly, because of their 'new' mission-critical status, marketing investments are attracting the serious attention of finance professionals. As part of a wider revolution in thinking about what kind of corporate assets are important in today's business environment, intangibles such as knowledge about customers and markets, or the power of brands, have assumed a new importance (Doyle 2000, Perrier 1997). The race is on to find robust methods of quantifying and evaluating such assets for the benefit of corporate managements and the wider investment community.

Unfortunately, this new focus on the importance of marketing has not improved the profile of marketing professionals. Instead, the spotlight has merely highlighted their weaknesses and shortcomings. After one 1997 survey (see Shaw 1998) on the perceived status of the profession, John Stubbs, CEO of the UK Marketing Council was forced to comment

> I was taken aback by just how little reputation marketing actually has among other functions ... marketing and marketers are not

respected by the people in their organisations for their contributions to business strategy, results or internal communication. We often do not know what or who is good or bad at marketing; our measurements are not seen as credible; our highest qualifications are not seen to have compatible status with other professions.

A survey at Cranfield (Baker S. 2000) during a two year period, has revealed that marketers are seen as 'slippery, expensive, unreliable and unaccountable'.

A study by Synesis (2000) confirmed that this perception of the marketing function has not changed very much in the intervening few years. Synesis found 'a self-confident profession with high self-esteem', which unfortunately had 'some way to go to convince (their colleagues) that marketing is as effective as it could be'.

What does 'value added' really mean?

The term 'value-added' is fast becoming the new mantra for the late 1990s/early 21st century business literature, and is often used quite loosely to indicate a business concept that is intended to exceed either customer or investor expectations, or both. However, from the point of view of this essay, it is important to realise that the term has its origin in a number of different management ideas, and is used in very specific ways by different sets of authors. Most of the ideas come from the US, and have originated in business school and consultancy research in the mid-1980s.

Value chain analysis

Firstly, there is Michael Porter's well-known concept of value-chain analysis (Porter 1985). Porter's concept of value added is an incremental one; he focuses on how successive activities change the value of goods and services as they pass through various stages of a value chain. Rigby (1998) explains

> Value chain analysis is used to identify potential sources of economic advantage. the analysis disaggregates a firm into its major activities in order to understand the behaviour of costs and the existing and potential sources of differentiation. It determines how the firm's own value chain interacts with the value chains of suppliers, customers and competitors. Companies gain competitive

advantage by performing some or all of these activities at lower cost or with greater differentiation than competitors.

Shareholder value analysis (SVA)

Secondly there is Alfred Rappaport's equally well-known research on shareholder value analysis (Rappaport 1986). Rappaport's concept of value added focuses less on processes than Porter, and acts more as a final gateway in decision-making, although it can be used at multiple levels within a firm. Rigby (1998) describes SVA as

> The process of analysing how decisions affect the net present value of cash to shareholders. The analysis measures a company's ability to earn more than its total cost of capital .... Within business units, SVA measures the value the unit has created by analysing cash flows over time. At the corporate level, SVA provides a framework for evaluating options for improving shareholder value by determining the tradeoffs between reinvesting in existing businesses, investing in new businesses and returning cash to stockholders.

There are a number of different ways of measuring shareholder value added, one of which, market value added (MVA), needs further explanation. Market value added is a measure first proposed by consultants Sterne Stewart (Stewart 1991), which compares the total shareholder capital of a company (including retained earnings) with the current market value of the company (capitalisation and debt). When one is deducted from the other, a positive result means value has been added, and a negative result means investors have lost out (Vause 1997). Within the literature, there is much discussion of the merits of this measure, versus another approach proposed by Sterne Stewart – EVA (economic value added).

However, from the point of view of marketing value added, Walters and Halliday (1997) usefully sum up the discussion thus:

> As aggregate measures and as relative performance indicators they have much to offer ... [but] how can the manager responsible for developing and/or implementing growth objectives [use them] to identify and select from alternative [strategic] options?

Market value added is one of a number of tools that analysts and the capital markets use to assess the value of a company. Marketing value added as a research topic focuses more directly on the processes of creating that value through effective marketing investments.

Customer value

A third way of looking at value added is the customer's perception of value. Unfortunately, despite exhaustive research by academics and practitioners around the world (e.g. Zeithamel 1988, Bonoma and Clark 1988, Clark 1999), this elusive concept has proved almost impossible to pin down. Zeithamel, for instance stated

> What constitutes [customer] value – even in a single product category – appears to be highly personal and idiosyncratic.

Nevertheless, the individual customer's perception of the extra value represented by different products and services cannot be easily dismissed: in the guise of measures such as customer satisfaction and customer loyalty it is known to be the essence of brand success, and the whole basis of the new science of relationship marketing.

Accounting value

Finally, there is the accountant's definition of value added: 'value added = sales revenue – purchases and services' (Vause 1997). Effectively, this is a snapshot picture from the annual accounts of how the revenue from a sales period has been distributed, and how much is left over for reinvestment after meeting all costs, including shareholder dividends. Although this figure will say something about the past viability of a business, in itself it does not provide a guide to future prospects.

One reason that the term 'value added' has come to be used rather carelessly is that all these concepts of value, although different, are not mutually exclusive. Porter's value chain analysis is one of several extremely useful techniques for identifying potential new competitive market strategies. Rappaport's SVA approach can be seen as a powerful tool which enables managers to cost out the long term financial implications of pursuing one or other of the competitive strategies which have been identified. Customer perceptions are clearly a major driver (or destroyer) of annual audited accounting value in all companies, whatever strategy is pursued.

However, most companies today accept that value added, as defined by their annual accounts, is really only a record of what they achieved in the past, and that financial targets in themselves are insufficient as business objectives. Many companies are now convinced that focusing on more intangible measures of value added such as brand equity, customer loyalty, or customer satisfaction are the new routes to achieving financial results.

Unfortunately, research has found that there is no neat, causal link between offering additional customer value and achieving value added on a balance sheet (see Shaw 1998, Clark 1999, Doyle 2000). That is, good ratings from customers about perceived value do not necessarily lead to financial success. Nor do financially-successful companies necessarily offer products and services which customers perceive as offering better value than competitors.

In order to explain the link that *does* exist between customer-orientated strategies and financial results, a far more rigorous approach to forecasting costs and revenues is required than is usual in marketing planning, coupled with a longer term perspective on the payback period than is possible on an annual balance sheet. This cash-driven perspective is the basis of the SVA approach, and can be used in conjunction with any marketing-strategy formulation process.

However, despite its apparent compatibility with existing planning systems, it is important to stress that adherents of the SVA approach believe that, after all the calculations have been made about the impact of different strategic choices, the final decision about which strategy to pursue should be the one which generates the most value (cash) for shareholders. This point of view adds a further dimension to the strategic debate, and is by no means universally accepted: there is a vigorous and ongoing debate in the literature as to whether increasing shareholder value should be the ultimate objective of a corporation (e.g. McTaggart et al. 1994, Rappaport 1998, Goyder 1998, Kennedy 2000).

Despite these arguments, there is no denying that during the last ten years SVA (or variants on the technique) has become the single most dominating corporate valuation perspective in developed western economies (Stewart 1991, McTaggart et al. 1994, Copeland et al. 1995). However, its popularity tends to be limited to the boardroom and the stock exchanges. Several recent surveys (e.g. CSF Consulting 2000, KPMG 1999) have found that less than 30 per cent of companies were pushing SVA-based management techniques down to an operational level, because of difficulties in translating cash targets into practical, day-to-day management objectives.

This is a pity because, apart from its widespread use at corporate level, the SVA approach particularly merits extensive attention of researchers interested in putting a value on marketing, as it allows marketing investments (or indeed any investments) to be valued over a much longer period of time than the usual one-year budget cycle.

Although common sense might argue that developing strong product or service offerings, and building up a loyal, satisfied customer base will usually require a series of 1–2 year investment plans in any business, nevertheless, such is the universal distrust of marketing strategies and forecasts, it is common practice in most companies to write off marketing as a cost within each year's budget. It is rare for such expenditure to be treated as an investment which will deliver results over a number of years (Ward 1999), but research shows that companies who are able to do this create a lasting competitive edge (McTaggart et al. 1994, Rappaport 1998, Doyle 2000).

Against this background, let us now do a brief review of the state of marketing after at least a 50 year life.

A brief review of the state of marketing

> Now it is a strange thing, but things that are good to have and days that are good to spend are soon told about and not much to listen to; while things that are uncomfortable, palpitating and even gruesome, may make a good tale and take a deal of telling anyway   *Source*: J.R.R. Tolkien (1995) *The Hobbit,* Harper-Collins Publishers, London.

Perhaps there is some point to all the recent intellectual whingeing about the state of marketing. So, before suggesting a way forward, let us make a very brief review of what we have achieved after over 50 years of marketing. Let us look at the three main constituent parts: practitioners, consultants, and academics.

Practitioners

As for practitioners, what better place to start than with the famous Peters and Waterman's 'In Search of Excellence', (1982). According to Richard Pascale (1990), of Peters and Waterman's original 43 excellent companies, only six were still excellent only eight years later.

Table 3.1 shows clearly that many of Britain's best performing companies during the decade up to 1990 subsequently collapsed.

Table 3.2 shows a real company, (disguised here) which apparently has performed extremely well over a five year period. Table 3.3, however, shows clearly that its performance is extremely poor when set in context.

Table 3.1   Britain's top companies (management today)

Year	Company[1]	Market value (£m)	ROI[2]	Subsequent performance[3]
1979	MFI	57	50	Collapsed
1980	Lasmo	134	97	Still profitable
1981	Bejam	79	34	Acquired
1982	Racal	940	36	Still profitable
1983	Polly Peck	128	79	Collapsed
1984	Atlantic Computers	151	36	Collapsed
1985	BSR	197	32	Still profitable
1986	Jaguar	819	60	Acquired
1987	Amstrad	987	89	Still profitable
1988	Body Shop	225	89	Still profitable
1989	Blue Arrow	653	135	Collapsed

1. Where a company has been top for more than 1 year, the next best company has been chosen in the subsequent year eg. Poly Peck was related top 1983, '84 and '85
2. Pre-tax profit as a percent of investment capital
3. This table is similar to a P&L with one important exception – **depreciation**, a standard item in any P&L has been replaced by **capital expenditure**, which does not appear in P&Ls.
Source: Professor Peter Doyle, Warwick University

Table 3.2   InterTech's five year performance

Performance (£ million)	Base year	1	2	3	4	5
Sales revenue	£254	£293	£318	£387	£431	£454
– Cost of goods sold	135	152	167	201	224	236
Gross contribution	£119	£141	£151	£186	£207	£218
– Manufacturing overhead	48	58	63	82	90	95
– Marketing & sales	18	23	24	26	27	28
– Research & development	22	23	23	25	24	24
Net profit	£16	£22	£26	£37	£50	£55
Return on sales (%)	6.3%	7.5%	8.2%	9.6%	11.6%	12.1%
Assets	£141	£162	£167	£194	£205	£206
Assets (% of sales)	56%	55%	53%	50%	48%	45%
Return on assets (%)	11.3%	13.5%	15.6%	19.1%	24.4%	26.7%

© Professor Malcolm McDonald, Cranfield School of Management

Table 3.3   Why market-growth rates are important
InterTech's 5 year market-based performance

Performance (£ million)	Base year	1	2	3	4	5
Market growth	18.3%	23.4%	17.6%	34.4%	24.0%	17.9%
InterTech sales growth (%)	12.8%	17.4%	11.2%	27.1%	16.5%	10.9%
Market share(%)	20.3%	19.1%	18.4%	17.1%	16.3%	14.9%
Customer retention (%)	88.2%	87.1%	85.0%	82.2%	80.9%	80.0%
New customers (%)	11.7%	12.9%	14.9%	24.1%	22.5%	29.2%
% dissatisfied customers	13.6%	14.3%	16.1%	17.3%	18.9%	19.6%
Relative product quality	+10%	+8%	+5%	+3%	+1%	0%
Relative service quality	+0%	+0%	−20%	−3%	−5%	−8%
Relative new product sales	+8%	+8%	+7%	+5%	+1%	−4%

© Professor Malcolm McDonald, Cranfield School of Management

Table 3.4 (Davidson 1998) also shows that one apparently high per-forming company is really poor when the kind of non-reportable items shown in the table are taken into account.

Table 3.5 shows the retention rate of a real company by segment, whilst Figure 3.1 (from a Cranfield database of leading European Companies using an anonymous Audience Response System) shows that, almost 10 years since the famous Reicheld and Sasser (1990) article, very few companies measure customer retention by segment.

Figures 3.2 and 3.3 (also from a Cranfield database of over 500 leading European companies over a five year period) show clearly that very few organisations measure market or customer profitability, in spite of the fact that it always has been the cost of dealing with customers after the 'product' leaves the 'factory' that determines profitability.

Figure 3.4 indicates what marketing information the financial com-munity needs to make sensible investment decisions. It also shows very clearly that very little of this is reported in annual accounts.

Turning briefly to the body of marketing knowledge that has been taught for over 50 years, Greenley's summary of research into the extent to which it is used (see Table 3.6) reveals a depressing picture, whilst Table 3.7 shows the author's observations on the weaknesses of over 200 marketing plans formally reviewed over a 10 year period.

Finally, and also from a Cranfield database, Figure 3.5 reveals a depress-ing honesty amongst senior marketing practitioners about their lack of knowledge about the financial impact of marketing expenditure.

In short, notwithstanding that the above represents a somewhat random and biased selection of examples of the state of practitioner

Table 3.4   Quality of profits

%	Virtuous plc (%)	Dissembler plc (%)
Sales revenue	100	100
Cost of goods sold	43	61
Profit margin	57	39
Advertising	11	3
R&D	5	–
Capital investment	7	2
Investment ratio	23	5
Operating expenses	20	20
Operating profit	14	14
Key trends →	• Past 5 year revenue growth 10% pa • Heavy advertising investment in new/ improved products • Premium priced products, new plant, so low cost of goods solds	• Flat revenue, declining volume • No recent product innovation, little advertising • Discounted pricing, so high cost of goods sold

The make-up of 14 per cent operating profits		
Factor	Virtuous plc (%)	Dissembler plc (%)
Profit on existing products over 3 years old	21	15
Losses on products recently launched or in development	(7)	(1)
Total operating profits	14	14

Source: Hugh Davidson's 'Even More Offensive Marketing', Butterworth-Heinemann, Oxford, 1998

marketing, most readers will in their heart of hearts recognise that they are not far from the truth.

Consultants

Turning secondly to consultants, which includes the likes of advertising agencies, they appear to have fared little better. The author has painstakingly listed over 300 consultant fads developed during the past 30 years, a small selection of which are listed in Table 3.8.

Table 3.5 Measurement of segment profitability

	Total market	Segment 1	Segment 2	Segment 3	Segment 4	Segment 5	Segment 6
Percentage of market represented by segment	100.0	14.8	9.5	27.1	18.8	18.8	11.0
Percentage of all profits in total market produced by segment	100.0	7.1	4.9	14.7	21.8	28.5	23.0
Ratio of profit produced by segment to weight of segment in total population	1.00	0.48	0.52	0.54	1.1	1.52	2.09
Defection rate	23%	20%	17%	15%	28%	30%	35%

Source: Cranfield Database: Payne, A. 1999

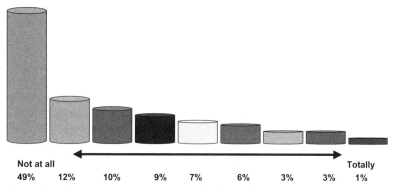

Figure 3.1   We measure customer retention by market segment
Source: Marketing Value Added Cranfield Conference, April 2002

To what extent do you allocate attributable costs (interface costs) to individual accounts (not marmalading costs across the whole customer base)?

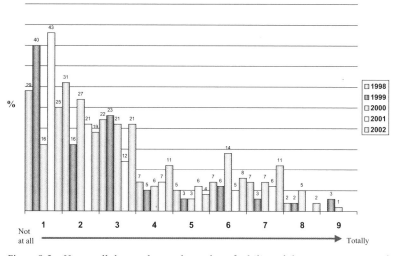

Figure 3.2   How well do you know the real profitability of the top ten accounts?
Source: Cranfield Key Account Management Research Club, 2002

During the past 10 years, many companies have sought a remedy for their declining fortunes by retreating into faddism, hungrily adopting one fad after another as they were peddled by eager consultants. In most cases these initiatives have failed, as organisations have treated

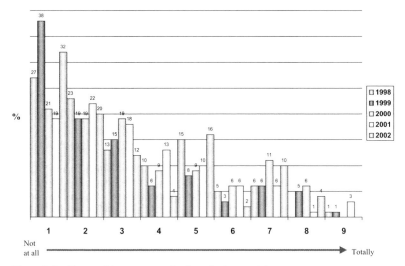

Figure 3.3 External investor marketing disclosure (a)
Source: Cranfield Key Account Management Research Club, 2002

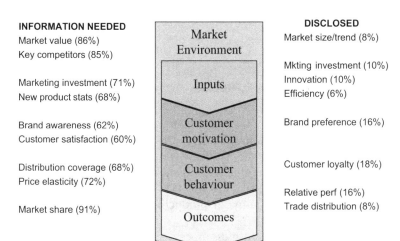

Figure 3.4 External investor marketing disclosure (b)
Source: Brand Finance 1999; Professor Hugh Davidson, (Cranfield visiting professor)

Table 3.6   Outline of previous research

Study	Country	Focus	Outline of results
Buzzell and Wiersema (1981)	USA	SP	Limited use of formal planning methods
McColl-Kennedy et al. (1989)	Australia	MP	Awareness and usage of methods – low
Greenley (1985)	UK	MP	Only 24% use portfolio analysis; half use PLC analysis
Haspeslagh (1982)	USA	SP	Only 45% use portfolio analysis regularly
Hopkins (1981)	USA	MP	A quarter use portfolio analysis only 13% use PLC analysis
Hooley et al. (1984)	UK	MP	Half use SWOT analysis, one-third use PLC, only a few use portfolio, PIMS, perceptual mapping and conjoint analysis
Reld and Hinkley (1989)	UK/ Hong Kong	SP	Little awareness of portfolio and PLC analysis, and PIMS
Ross and Silverplatt (1987)	USA	SP	Half use porfolio analysis regularly, and a quarter use PIMS regularly
Verhage and Waarts (1988)	Netherlands	MP	15% use portfolio analysis, 27% use PLC with 62% using SWOT
Wittink and Cattin (1989)	USA	MP	Limited use of conjoint analysis by MR consultants
Wood and LaForge (1986)	USA	SP	Portfolio analysis used by 67% of sample

Source: Greenley (1994)
MP, marketing planning; SP, strategic planning

them as a quick-fix bolt-on without addressing their underlying problems. The International Standards Organisation's ISO 9000 quality initiative, for example, very laudable when used sensibly, has, in the main, only been a guarantee that organisations can produce rubbish perfectly and consistently. We use the word 'rubbish' judiciously, because there is little point in producing perfectly something that people do not buy.

Another fad has been business process re-engineering (BPR). This has been an outstanding success in those companies which have used it to redesign their processes to create value for customers. But in those organisations which have not grasped the nettle of customer satisfaction, it has achieved merely cosmetic productivity improvements (Edwards and Peppard 1997). Yet another has been balanced score-

Table 3.7   Key areas for improvements in strategic marketing plans

---

- Market overviews contain substantially more information than is necessary, with no hint of the implications for marketing activity.
- Key segments are rarely identified. 'Segments' are often sectors or products, rather than groups of customers with similar needs.
- The competitive situation is not well analysed and plans appear to assume no activity or reaction by competitors.
- SWOT analyses rarely pin down convincingly the value that is required by segments. They are frequently too general to lead to any actionable prepositions.
- Our own distinctive competences are rarely isolated and built on.
- SWOTs are rarely summarised clearly and logically in a portfolio which provides a categorisation of the relative potential of each and our relative strengths in each.
- Marketing objectives are frequently confused with marketing strategies and do not follow logically from the portfolio summary.
- The resource implications of effecting the marketing plans are not always clear.

Based on formal critiques of strategic marketing plans from the SBUs of multinational, industrial and service businesses, McDonald, M., Cranfield Database, May 1996

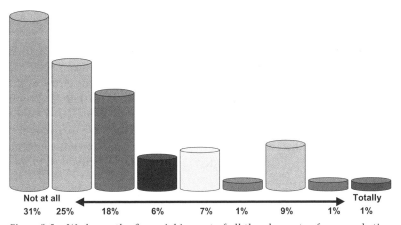

Not at all								Totally
31%	25%	18%	6%	7%	1%	9%	1%	1%

Figure 3.5   We know the financial impact of all the elements of our marketing strategy and we measure and report them to the board
Source: Cranfield Marketing Value Added Research Club, April 2002

cards. This too, for CEOs who understand the need to balance the requirements of all the stakeholders in a company delivering customer value, has been very successful. It is a strategy used with great success by BAA, for example, for managing its complex web of stakeholder

Table 3.8   Fads (300)

- In search of excellence
- Marketing warfare
- One minute manager
- MBWA
- Skunk works
- 7 Ss
- Etc.

---

relationships. But for those CEOs who do not understand the import-ance of being market driven, it has proved to be just another fad.

Of course all of these initiatives are fabulous and do work, but only when they are seen in the context of providing superior customer value as a means of providing superior shareholder value. Alas, even in those organisations committed to 'relationship' and 'one-to-one' marketing, too often customers remain the Cinderellas. As Harvard Business School's Susan Fournier et al. has pointed out (1998), rapid development of relationship techniques in the USA has been accompanied by growing customer dissatisfaction. The much vaulted relationship that companies were so eager to forge with their customers involved not so much delighting them as abusing them, suggested Fournier et al.

The problem is that companies have become so internally focused they have got carried away with supply-side issues and taken their eye off the customer ball. Until organisations make a serious effort to lift their heads above the parapet and understand their markets and their customers better, all the great initiatives referred to above will amount to expensive, time-consuming mistakes. Most boards are spending too much of their valuable time on internal operational efficiency (doing things right) at the expense of external operational effectiveness (doing the right things).

In conclusion, whilst consultants have not surprisingly fared some-what better than the marketing practitioner community, they could hardly be adjudged to have had a big impact on practice.

Academics

Finally, of course, there is the academic community. Table 3.9 lists a small selection of quotations from well-known academics. Most damning of all is the last one. At the Academy of Marketing Debate in the summer of 2000, the author carefully prepared his debate-winning

Table 3.9   Academics and marketing practice

- 'Much research is directed at technical refinement, which produces low risk, quick win publications that are largely irrelevant or incomprehensible to practitioners. The voice of academics is becoming weaker' (Hugh Wilmott of MBS)
- Robin Wensley said that marketing academics have had little impact. 'A much wider understanding of the nature of the competitive market place is required, given that it is such a central phenomenon'
- Of ten issues, (confirmed by 3 academic papers and the MSI), only 4% were addressed in the top, 5 star rated academic journals

---

Source: McDonald, M. Academy of Marketing Debate, University of Derby, 2000

proposal that the academic marketing community was out of touch with marketing practice. One of the facts gathered concerned the number of papers in marketing academic communities which addressed the top 14 issues of concern to practitioners (Wensley 2000) in the two top, five-star rated academic journals. Four per cent was the derisory number! One wonders whether there is a grain of truth in the assertion that academics are being increasingly forced by the RAE to write for a narrow, esoteric audience in media which are of little relevance to the real world.

Whilst such journals clearly have relevance to academics and whilst their role is fully appreciated, the influence and prestige afforded to them by the RAE is out of all proportion to the problems facing the global marketing community and only succeeds in diverting the abundant genius in our academic community into a cul-de-sac. Furthermore, the style of such pieces is also becoming increasingly dense and impenetrable. The author's spoof piece in Table 3.10 is a somewhat lighthearted parody of what senior academics face when reviewing certain papers for double blind refereed journals.

The net impact of this sad neglect by the academic and practitioner communities is that marketing as a function has been increasingly relegated away from the core strategy-making engine of organisations to become a sales support department, in charge of T-shirts and promotion.

From tactics to strategy

So, what can be done to begin to recover from the sorry state the marketing community finds itself in?

Firstly, we have to work hard to recapture the high ground – the strategy domain. This, however, means reaching some kind of

Table 3.10 Critique of new MBA Module

In undertaking an in-depth perusal of the evolutionary interaction of this acronymic organisational communication, the dual orientation for the analysis paradoxically required an unashamed repositioning of the eclectic conceptual frame work amongst the multi-disciplinary body of illuminative speculation in predominantly scholarly bureaucratisation.

Yet, coincidentally, its empirical complexity had to remain relevant to the esoteric realities of postmodern professional integrative antecedent development trends at appropriately conceptualised and operationally-implemented meta levels.

Consequently, it was necessary to review the independently formulated psyhometric traditions and to employ confidently the articulatedly-present phenomenological methodologies currently available for polysyllabic paradigm exploration. Unfortunately, the ensuing generalised multifaceted model for evaluation (in its specific systems dimension, naturally) had unexpectedly and unexplainably exploded – though not exhaustively. The major administrative atomistic components, suitably enumerated, are now, unfortunately, somewhat hindering the Assessor's understanding process. However, tabula-tion analysis of the topography implicitly indicates that comprehensive evalu-ation of the interdenominational micro data has finally exhausted the course Assessor and any further critical, unbiased, postmodernistical review, will just have to wait until he has had a few strong gin and tonics!

I suspect you may not know what this means, but I don't really care, even if it takes you half an hour to decode it!

I call this style *'anorexia doctoratitis'* – an excessive desire to be more and more impressive verbally, leading to mental emaciation and, eventually, death.

Source: McDonald, M. Open University Business School, Critique of a new MBA Module on Postmodern Marketing, 2001

consensus about what marketing is. Enormous damage is done to our cause when the President of The Chartered Institute of Marketing declares: *'Marketing isn't a function. It is an attitude of mind'* (Thompson D. 2001). There will be many amongst us who wonder how an attitude of mind can be measured, researched, developed, protected, examined, etc., all of these being the avowed purpose of the professional body. Add to this the hundreds of different definitions of marketing to be found in books and papers on marketing and the confusion is complete. A selection of 30 such definitions are to be found in McDonald 2002, most of which involve doing things to customers.

Let us be unequivocal about marketing. Just like finance, or HR, or IT, it is a *function*, but described in terms of what it actually entails, as shown in Table 3.11. This is shown diagrammatically in Figure 3.6.

Figure 3.6 shows a consolidated summary of the marketing process.

Table 3.11   Definition of marketing

Marketing is a process for:
- defining markets
- quantifying the needs of the customer groups (segments) within these markets
- putting together the value propositions to meet these needs, communicating these value propositions to all those people in the organisation responsible for delivering them and getting their buy-in to their role
- playing an appropriate part in delivering these value propositions (usually only communications)
- monitoring the value actually delivered.

For this process to be effective, organisations need to be consumer/customer-driven

Source: McDonald, M. Marketing Plans: how to prepare them; how to use them, Butterworth–Heinemann, 2002

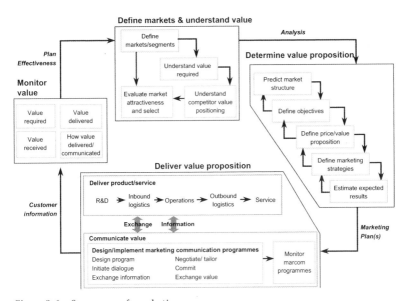

Figure 3.6   Summary of marketing map

It will be seen that boxes 1 and 2 are clearly about strategy determination, whilst boxes 3 and 4 are about tactical implementation and measurement. It is these latter two that have come to represent marketing as a function, which is still principally seen as sales support and promotion. The author recently drove through a new housing estate, where a neon sign above an up-market prefab blasted out the following words: *'The Marketing Suite'*, loosely translated as: *'This is where you come to get sold to'*. And when government bodies, charities and the like say *'we need marketing'*, what they mostly mean is *'we need some promotion'*.

The options, then, are clear. Firstly, let us all stop this pretence at strategy and concentrate on where the marketing community actually is, which is sales support. Or let us take marketing centre stage, with a major impact on corporate strategy development.

There is more than enough evidence (see, for example, Jenkins and McDonald 1997) that one of the fundamental determinants of corporate success – i.e. correct market definition, market segmentation and positioning is poorly understood in the corporate world at large. So, let us begin by looking in a little more detail at each of the boxes in Figure 3.7.

This process is clearly cyclical, in that monitoring the value delivered will update the organisation's understanding of the value that is required by its customers. The cycle may be predominantly an annual one, with a marketing plan documenting the output from the 'understand value' and 'develop value proposition' processes, but equally changes throughout the year may involve fast iterations around the cycle to respond to particular opportunities or problems.

We have used the term 'Determine value proposition', to make plain that we are here referring to the decision-making process of deciding what the offering to the customer is to be – what value the customer will receive, and what value (typically the purchase price and on-going revenues) the organisation will receive in return. The process of delivering this value, such as by making and delivering a physical product or by delivering a service, is covered by 'Deliver value proposition'.

Thus, it can be seen that the first two boxes are concerned with strategic planning processes (in other words, developing market strategies), whilst the third and fourth boxes are concerned with the actual delivery in the market of what was planned and then measuring the effect. Throughout, we use the word 'proposition' to indicate the nature of the offer from the organisation to the market.

It is well known that not all of the value proposition delivering processes will be under the control of the marketing department, whose role varies considerably between organisations. The marketing department should be responsible for and central to the first two processes, 'Understand value' and 'Determine value proposition', although even these need to involve numerous functions, albeit co-ordinated by specialist marketing personnel. The 'Deliver value' process is the role of the whole company, including for example product development, manufacturing, purchasing, sales promotion, direct mail, distribution, sales and customer service.

The various choices made during this marketing process are constrained and informed not just by the outside world, but also by the organisation's asset base. Whereas an efficient new factory with much spare capacity might underpin a growth strategy in a particular market, a factory running at full capacity would cause more reflection on whether price should be used to control demand, unless the potential demand warranted further capital investment. As well as physical assets, choices may be influenced by financial, human resources, brand and information technology assets, to name just a few. (For a detailed explanation of each of the four boxes, see McDonald M. 2002).

Marketing's role in value creation

There is, however, one final, but crucial piece of the jigsaw to put in place. Table 3.12 states clearly that marketing can and should have a central role to play in creating sustainable competitive advantage.

Figure 3.7 shows a typical array from any stock exchange of the relationship between risk and return, the diagonal line being the Beta.

Any firm on the line will normally be making industry average returns for its shareholders – in other words, making returns equal to the weighted average cost of capital (WACC). Firms making consistent returns greater then the WACC is creating shareholder wealth, known generally as Shareholder Value Added, Economic Value Added, positive net present value, super profits, sustainable competitive advantage and so on. Figure 3.8 shows diagrammatically how sustainable competitive advantage can be achieved.

As Doyle has pointed out (2000), modern finance is based on four principles:

- cash flow (the basis of value)
- the true value of money

Table 3.12 The purpose of strategic marketing planning

The overall purpose of strategic marketing, and its principal focus is the identification and creation of sustainable competitive advantage

© Professor Malcolm McDonald, Cranfield School of Management

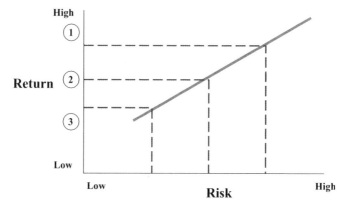

Figure 3.7 Financial risk and return
Source: Adapted from Sri Srikanthan, Cranfield School of Management

Figure 3.8 The route to sustainable competitive advantage (SCA)
Source: Professor Malcolm McDonald, Cranfield School of Management

- the opportunity cost of capital (other investments of a similar risk)
- the concept of net present value (the sum of the net cash flows discounted by the opportunity cost of capital)

Also, he pointed out that, whilst accountants do not measure intangible assets, the discrepancy between market and book values shows that investors do. Hence, expenditures to develop marketing assets make sense of the sum of the discounted cash flow they generate as positive.

A little thought will indicate that every single corporate activity, whether it be R&D, IT, purchasing or logistics, is ultimately reflected in the relative value put on a firm's offer by its customers. The marketing function, as defined in Figure 3.6, (but particularly the strategic roles outlined in boxes 1 and 2) is central to this, as every one of the four, (or five, six or seven Ps) can only be improved by the *whole* organisation focussing its attention on its customers.

What should marketing be doing ?

The crux of the matter is a failure to align marketing activities with fundamental shareholder value objectives. Marketing objective setting is, in practice, murky or, at worst, downright wrong. Increasing sales volume, the most widely cited marketing objective, can easily be achieved by sacrificing profitability, for instance. Increasing profit, another commonly cited marketing objective can be also attained in the short-term by relinquishing investments for future growth.

Perhaps more worrying than comments about lack of alignment between marketing strategies and corporate objectives are charges of poor marketing professionalism. There is widespread evidence from research (McDonald 1996) and other business schools that very few marketing professionals, actually understand or know how to use the widely available strategic analysis tools that would help them to dovetail their plans with what is going on in the wider marketplace, and elsewhere in their organisations.

There are numerous tried and tested tools that would be of immediate value in improving marketing's contribution to the main board agenda. For example:

- Financial rigour in appraising marketing objectives would be a useful start. Financial managers have used tools such as DCF (discounted cash flow analysis) for at least 40 years to support investment appraisal and resource allocation. DCF is not complicated, and it requires little more than a PC spreadsheet. However these methods are mainly applied to capital projects and mergers and acquisitions. Although DCF is occasionally used to calculate brand valuations, it is not widely used to support marketing decision making. Now frequently referred to as NPV (net present value), it is still in widespread use by accountants for capital projects.
- Marketing planning methods should be more strategic. Unfortunately, the annual budget cycle has a stranglehold over marketing objective

setting. Over 20 studies of the marketing planning processes during a 15 year period reveal that less than 20 per cent of marketing professionals use strategic objective setting methods. Objectives are predominantly short-term and have little connection with wider corporate plans for growing shareholder value.

- Resource allocation needs to be aligned with business growth. Yet there is a widespread disconnection between marketing's growth objectives, and corporate cost cutting objectives. Symptoms of this disconnection can be observed in the extremely poor service provided by the majority of call centres, and the inadequate customer response from many Internet business ventures, which are very often set up as corporate cost-cutting initiatives. Again, the treatment is conceptually easy. Yet surprisingly few marketing plans adequately assess their resource implications (especially not cross-functionally).
- Market segmentation should be driven by customer needs and wants, according to best-practice studies. These techniques are well understood in the academic world, but corporate practice still seems to be in the dark ages. Yet segmentation in practice is dominated by easily available demographic data, rather than more difficult-to-obtain data on actual customer behaviour and attitudes.
- Customer profitability is also known to be a key driver of shareholder value, according to academic studies. Again the state of marketing practice is poor. Remarkably few organisations use this vital tool.
- Customer retention analysis, and root-cause customer defection analysis, are widely written about. Market research firms can offer extensive data on retention and loyalty. Once more the take-up is pitifully low.

The low value that marketing places on measurement is brought home by looking at what marketing spends today on market research – about £500m annually in the UK. Compare this with the amount engineers spend on research and development – over 100 times what marketing spends on research. Or compare it with the amount one oil company recently spent on a new financial information system – £500m – the same figure that all UK companies spend on marketing information.

Having given a brief introduction to the need for marketers to undertake a fundamental reappraisal of marketing metrics, the author has developed a process for auditing the main elements of marketing investments and for linking these investments to shareholder wealth. We have named this process 'Marketing Due Diligence' in order to indicate that marketing should be treated in exactly the same way as, for example, an organisation's financial audit, with the board, through their marketers, held accountable for the investments made in building shareholder value.

The purpose of a financial audit, which is a legal requirement, is to ensure financial due diligence and, whilst the ENRON scandal demonstrates that it doesn't always work as it should, in the main, the financial audit process has served the business community well.

It is clear, however, that the time has come for a similar process of due diligence to be initiated for marketing processes. However, this essay is not the place to set out this detailed process, but readers who are interested can obtain details by emailing Professor McDonald at m.mcdonald@cranfield.ac.uk

References

Baker, S. (2000) *Defining a Marketing Paradigm – the view of senior non-marketers*, Academy of Marketing Conference, Derby University Proceedings.

Bonoma, T.V. and Clark, B.H. (1988) *Marketing Performance Assessment*, Harvard Business School 1988.

Clark, B.H. (1999) *Marketing Performance Measures: History and Interrelationships*, J. Marketing Management, Vol. 15, Issue 8, pp. 711–732.

Copeland, T., Koller, T. and Murrin, J. (2000) *Valuation: Measuring and Managing the Value of Companies*, 2E 1995, 3E John Wiley & Sons.

CSF Consulting (2000) *Managing for Value: Survey of Current Practice*, March.

Davidson, H. (1997) *Even More Offensive Marketing*, London: Penguin.

Doyle, P. (1998) *Marketing Management & Strategy*, First Edition 1994, Second Edition, New Jersey: Prentice Hall.

Doyle, P. (2000) *How Shareholder Value Analysis Re-defines Marketing*, Market Leader, pp. 16–25, Spring.

Edwards, C. and Peppard, J. (1997) 'Operationalising Strategy Through Process', Long Range Planning, Vol. 30, No. 5, 753–756.

Fournier, S., Dobscha, S. and Mick, D.G. (1998) 'Preventing the Premature Death of Relationship Marketing', Harvard Business Review, Jan–Feb 98, Vol. 76, Issue 1, pp. 42–50.

Goyder, M. (1998) *Living Tomorrow's Company*, London: Nicholas Brealey.

Greenley, G. (1994) 'Marketing Planning in UK and US Companies', Journal of Strategic Marketing, Vol. 2, No. 2, 140–154.

Jenkins, M. and McDonald, M. (1997) 'Market Segmentation: organisational archetypes and research agendas', European Journal of Marketing, Vol. 31, No. 1, 17–32.

Kennedy, A. (2000) *The End of Shareholder Value*, Orion 2000.

KPMG (1999) *Value Based Management: The Growing Importance of Shareholder Value in Europe*, KPMG Consulting.

McDonald, M. (2000) Academy of Marketing Debate, University of Derby.

McDonald, M. (1996) 'Strategic Marketing Planning: theory; practice; and research agendas', Journal of Marketing Management, Jan–April 96, Vol. 12, Issue 1–3, pp. 5–27.

McDonald, M. (2002) 'Marketing Plans: how to prepare them; how to use them', Butterworth–Heinemann, Oxford.

McTaggart, J.M., Kontes, P.W. and Mankins, M.C. (1994) *The Value Imperative*, Free Press.

Pascale, R.T. (1990) 'Managing on the Edge', Simon and Schuster, New York.

Perrier, R. (1997) (Ed.) *Brand Valuation*, Second Edition, Premier Books.

Peters, T.J. and Waterman, R.H. (1982) 'In Search of Excellence', Warner Books, New York.

Piercy, N. (1999) Chapter 21 *Marketing implementation, organisational change and internal marketing strategy*, in Baker, M. (Ed.), The Marketing Book, 4E, Butterworth Heinemann: London.

Porter, M.E. (1985) *Competitive Advantage: Creating and Sustaining Superior Performance*, Free Press: New York.

Rappaport, A. (1998) *Creating Shareholder Value*, Free Press: New York. Revised Edition 1998.

Reicheld, F.F. and Sasser, W.E., Jr. (1990) 'Zero Defections: Quality Comes to Services' Harvard Business Review, Sept–Oct 90, Vol. 68, Issue 5, pp. 105–111.

Rigby, D.K. (1998) *Management Tools and Techniques*, Bain & Co: London.

Shaw, R., McDonald, M. and White, C. (2002) *Marketing Value Added Literature Review*, The Cranfield MVA Research Club.

Shaw, R. and Mazur, L. (1997) *Marketing Accountability*, FT Management Reports.

Shaw, R. (1998) *Improving Marketing Effectiveness*, London: Economist Books.

Stewart, G.B. (1997) *The Quest for Value*, Harper Business: Chicago.

Stone, M., Woodcock, N. and Machtynger, L. (2000) *Customer Relationship Marketing*, Kogan Page: London.

Synesis (2000) *A Report on the Future of Marketing*, Synesis 2000.
(Synesis are a firm of marketing consultants. Try http://www.synesis.co.uk/ for more information/contact details, etc.)

Thompson, D. (2001) Keynote speech, Annual Fellows Dinner, Cookham, Chartered Institute of Marketing.

Vause, R. (1997) *Guide to Analysing Companies*, Economist Books: London.

Walters, D. and Halliday, M. (1997) *Marketing & Finance: Working the Interface*, Allen & Unwin: London.

Ward, K. (1989) *Financial Aspects of Marketing*, Butterworth Heinemann: London.

Ward, K. (1999) Chapter 20 *Controlling Marketing*, in Baker, M. (Ed.), The Marketing Book, 4E, Butterworth Heinemann: London.

Wensley, R. (2000) 'The MSI Priorities: a critical review on researching firm performance, customer experience and marketing', Journal of Marketing Management, Jan–Apr 2000, Vol. 16, Issue 1–3, pp. 11–27.

Wilson, H. (1996) *An Investigation into the Impact of Decision Support Systems on Strategic Marketing Planning Practice*, A Cranfield University PhD.

Zeithamel, V.A. (1988) *Consumer Perceptions of Price, Quality and Value*, Journal of Marketing, July 88, Vol. 52, Issue 3, pp. 2–22., Reprinted in Enis, B.M. et al. (Eds), Marketing Classics, 8th Edition, Prentice Hall: London.

4
Innovation and Sustainable Competitive Advantage

Dale Littler

'He that will not apply new remedies must expect new evils; for time is the greatest innovator' Francis Bacon (1625): 'Of Innovations' in *Essays*.

Introduction

Innovation is heralded is as the essential ingredient of any organisation's strategic formula. The reason is quite simple: organisations are faced with significant changes that can ultimately undermine the bases on which they operate. There are countless examples where organisations have failed to detect market adjustments, alterations and disruptions that have ultimately acted to generate significant declines in market share, sales and profitability. The need for change often remains unrecognised, or is approached incrementally when more short-term radical action is required, or is overtly resisted because current experiences are regarded as exceptional. Only an impending or actual crisis in for example organisational performance, such as a major decline in profitability over a period, leads to the significant readjustments that the changes in its organisational context demanded. Reuters, a provider of information to others in the financial services industry found that its failure to take account of innovation and increasing competition resulted in significant losses.

There are other positive reasons why organisations need to consider innovation. Innovation potentially enables the organisation not only to take charge of the strategic agenda, but it is also a source of incremental revenue and profits. Innovation is a means of securing a quasi monopoly position that if expeditiously exploited can be a substantial source of growth.

Reuters

Reuters, a major provider of financial information, has been suffering from a significant decline in market share and revenues that have in turn resulted in losses. Since July 2001, the Company has announced plans to reduce its workforce by 5500. The Company, which was founded in 1851, has for many years dominated the financial data sector. It has however been losing out to its much younger rival, Bloomberg, which has now over-taken Reuters in terms of revenue share. Compared to a range of products offered to different segments, Bloomberg offers just one product aimed at the premium segment of the market. Reuter's products were old fashioned, using complex specialists operating systems, rather than Windows-style products familiar to most computer users. Bloomberg on the other hand provided messaging services and its terminals came with analytical tools, giving for example not only the price of the bond, but the bond's price history and its performance compared with other investments. Reuters also found that the Internet disintermediarised the supply of financial information and undermined their role. Also, Reuters dominated the wrong sector of the market: it had a powerful share of the trading floors where dealers use its systems to price securities and currencies, but as investment banks merged, the number of traders and hence the number of screens declined. Reuters has been forced to respond to Bloomberg's innovations but in the meantime Bloomberg has emerged as a formidable competitor, and is now the market leader.

Sources: Author, derived from Shah S. (2003), and *The Economist* (2003)

Innovation however has many guises; it can involve varying degrees of change in the organisation, its technologies and its markets, it is risky, and it is often surrounded by a thick fog of uncertainty, that together with the attended disruptions it is seen as generating, unsurprisingly can lead to preference for the tried over the unknown. Fear of the new generates a strong preference for the familiar.

Here then I explore innovation and how it can be exploited to obtain the prize of a sustainable competitive advantage. First I consider the context of competition and how innovation stimulates rivalry and customer choices. I then proceed to assess the influences of competitiveness and how innovation itself makes a significant contribution. This is followed by a consideration of whether or not it is possible to secure a sustainable competitive advantage. I conclude that because competition is an unending race, sustainable competitiveness is the outcome of a constant emphasis on customer-focused innovation. Finally I explore how organisations might enhance their success in innovation by conscientiously adopting a customer-focused approach.

Competition

Most organisations operate within a dynamic competitive environment that is driven by innovation, customer choices and rivalry. These form the triangle of competition (see Figure 4.1).

Competition is often presented as a process of rivalry between independently acting organisations that are striving to secure privileged access to resources and customers. This rivalry not only occurs between businesses in similar product markets; it can arise from businesses operating in other markets, while there is also the potential of competition from yet unknown sources that can act to stimulate organisations to develop and shake off complacency:

> It is hardly necessary to point out that competition of the kind we now have in mind acts not only when in being but also when it is merely an ever present threat. It disciplines before it attacks. The businessman feels himself to be in a competitive situation even if he is alone in the field.   (Schumpeter 1950: 85)

In many product markets, especially those facing insignificant growth, there is much tit-for-tat rivalry, with organisations responding to the actions of competitors. Any advantage obtained is generally temporary because it is later eroded by the subsequent reactions of their rivals.

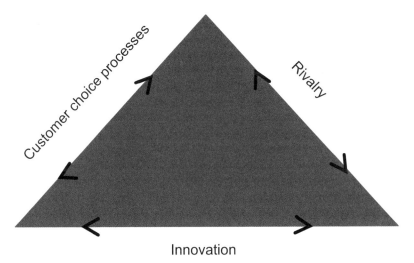

Figure 4.1   The triangle of competition

The major challenge is to break out of this mould of zero-sum competition through developing new markets, entering growing product markets, where it is possible for many if not all competitors to achieve medium term benefits, or achieving some major breakthrough in existing markets. Innovation is a major means of achieving both these positions.

The second component of the competition triangle is customer choice processes: the manner in which customers make decisions, the factors which affect those decisions, and the changing importance of those influences. It is the ability of organisations to understand the dynamics of both existing and potential customers' decision processes that will affect their relative positioning in the market. Those businesses which are, in essence, able to effect empathy with customers are likely to have a powerful competitive advantage. Gaining this appreciation of customers and their changing tastes and preferences requires, as we shall see, deep and somewhat novel customer research methodologies.

The third aspect of the competition triangle is innovation: the process by which organisations modify, reshape, adjust and alter their offerings in a way that not only reflects extant changes in the markets within which these organisations operate, but also anticipates effectively the manner in which consumer preferences will change in the light of what it and its competitors might do.

Competitiveness

It is the sensitivity to change in its markets and the capacity to adapt accordingly that are the hallmarks of the competitive organisation. The ability to compete effectively may itself by a function of several factors: efficiency; marginal differentiation; proprietariness; and flexibility that collectively form the square of competitiveness as shown in Figure 4.2.

Marginal differentiation

Although differentiation is regarded as a major generic competitive strategy, it embraces almost all means of securing a competitive advantage. Differentiation in itself is not the goal. Rather it is differentiation along parameters that are valued as important by target customers. Moreover the offerings have to be perceived by these customers as beneficially different along these dimensions from those of the competition. These differences only have to be sufficient to generate customer preferences for the product at a price that optimises

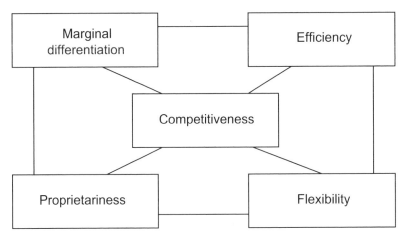

Figure 4.2   The competitiveness square

revenue. The organisation is not necessarily aiming for the **best** technology, product design, quality of packaging, or functionality unless these are necessary to persuade customers to exercise their preferences in favour of the company's offering. Investing to secure the maximum advantage may not be essential in the first instance, and it may even be strategically important to hold back some differentiation, as it were, to enable the business to react effectively to the inevitable reactions of competitors. The challenge of balancing the customer desired level of differentiation against the tendency to strive for excellence is starkest in the case of technology where developments are often shaped by the enthusiasm of the technologists rather than by a considered analysis of customer desires and behaviour. Customers are not generally driven by the need to have what technologists regard as a superior technology; indeed they may not even be interested in the technology itself, but rather in what the product does, how easy it is to use, how convenient it is to purchase, the value for money they see it offering, the level of service support, and the wide availability of complementary products.

Efficiency

A second major contributor to competitiveness is efficiency. In accepted views of competition, price is assumed to be a major factor influencing demand with the result that the focus is on cost. Where there is intense rivalry the most efficient will ultimately survive. However, it is evident that price is not always a major influencer of customer choice processes. For example, in the case of highly innovative offerings, customers may well be prepared to pay premium prices for the novel features offered and the lack of competition in the early phases at least means that the innovator is able to capitalise on this. The strategic focus is often on establishing a defined market position and maintaining or even increasing this as the market grows. As the product market develops, there will be imitation, the best practice businesses will tend to grow faster, and by various means squeeze out other businesses. It may also be that even in more mature markets customers seek benefits, additional to those in the basic product, for which they are prepared to pay. However, the process of competition generally results in convergence of those organisations that survive towards some form of standard: incremental changes are inevitably matched by rivals if they wish to remain in the market and the provision of additional none tangible product features become necessary for survival. It is the efficiency with which the total offering is produced and marketed, and indeed of the means of incrementally developing it, that becomes an essential condition for survival as the product market develops. It is evident that even if efficiency is not of prime concern during the embryonic phases of market development, it becomes increasingly relevant as the best practice firms squeeze out the less efficient. Moreover, with the onset of maturity differentiation is more difficult to attain and, even when an advantage is secured, to retain, and price can assume an increasing, if not the major, importance. Those firms that are the most efficient in what they do are more strongly positioned to manage the vagaries of the environment.

Proprietariness

A third interlinked element of the square is proprietariness: the ability to capture exclusively the benefits of the efficiency and differentiation that the competitive business has so eagerly sought. The ability to secure a sustainable competitive advantage is the holy grail of competitiveness that may, as we shall discuss below, be difficult to realise in practice. The fickleness of customer preferences together with the strategies adopted by existing and future rivals suggest that businesses may have to adopt a range of coping strategies. Some organisations may adopt policies aimed at enabling them to establish protected and significant leads demanding lengthy response times from competitors; others may focus on market segments and on providing offerings for them that have proved unattractive to incumbent firms. Others may engage in constant innovation, even planning the next generation of products before predecessors are launched, the process being impelled by the rapid pace of technological change and the ease with which many innovations can be imitated. Yet others may focus on gaining customers at an early stage and building in considerable switching costs. From the outset, it is evident that the firm engaged in innovation needs to address the issue of how it retains any proprietary position that its innovative stance awards.

Flexibility

The final side of the competitiveness square is flexibility. Competition involves change that is stimulated by the rivalry that is intrinsic to the process. Businesses are operating in a theatre of uncertainty, anticipating the consequences of their own actions, let alone the actions and implications of others, is problematic. Longer-term competitiveness rests on having openness to now knowing, adopting heuristics that accept uncertainties, and preparing for the unpredictable. Although the latter may involve developing strategies for different outcomes, by definition it is impossible to foresee all the range of possible eventualities. This suggests that organisations need to retain as much as possible the freedom to respond to what emerges. They should strive to avoid entering into large scale commitments especially at an early stage. Rather they might invest in a portfolio of diverse innovative developments, focus on module based product designs and manufacturing systems, and view innovative opportunities as options in which they take a stake with further investments only being made on the basis of continuing favourable outcomes. The requirement of flexibility certainly implies having a sound innovative capability: the skills and resources to be able to react effectively to the developments of others, while at the same time maintaining an intelligent sensitivity to the potential impact on existing activities of developments elsewhere.

Sustainable competitive advantage

It is evident that a major strategic question is: how do businesses in this rapidly changing environment sustain their competitiveness?

As has been noted a firm's competitiveness is fundamentally based on having a perceived difference that customers value. It can, however, be founded on many, diverse resources including the knowledge and experience embedded in the organisation's employees, a well established renowned reputation, favourable access to markets, and the possession of patents, contracts and trade secrets.

In order to be 'sustainable' these resources must be unique to the firm, not knowable by competitors and not easily transferable to others. Such resources can be difficult to imitate for a variety of reasons. For instance, the firm's access to its resources is based on unique historical conditions such as the manner in which it was founded, or its location which has provided it with access to scarce human skills (Hall 1992). Thus the firm may have a 'head start' in the market or have been able to secure enforceable property rights. There may also be causal ambiguity (Barney 1991). This occurs when the reasons for the firm's superior performance cannot be clearly articulated because the reasons for the link between its resources and its advantage are not clearly understood. Finally, there can be social complexity. The cause of its advantage may rest on complex social phenomena such as the interrelationships between managers, or its relationships and reputation with suppliers. Moreover, it may be that there are not available or it is not possible to develop substitutes for the firm's unique resources (Barney 1991). Of course a rival is able to substitute a similar resource even though it cannot match the firm's original resource exactly. Thus a company may through a unique combination of its resources have developed an innovation that is highly patent protected. However the firms very success may stimulate competitors to develop alternative technologies that offer at least similar customer benefits.

It is obvious that if a firm's competencies that are known to contribute to competitive advantage can be articulated and transferred easily within the firm then of course it may prove difficult to keep this understanding embedded in the firm. Competitors may be able to gain the requisite understanding by hiring managers from the firm or even engage in a form of industrial espionage. However, if causal ambiguity exists, the firm itself may not be cognisant of what provides its competitive advantage and therefore not be able to capitalise fully on it. Leveraging of the competencies under such conditions is obviously problematic.

Moreover, what provides a current competitive advantage may not be relevant in the future: any organisation will be confronted with significant changes brought about by technological, organisational or other forms of innovation that can alter, even negate, the bases on which the firm's competitive advantage is constructed. These innovations may engender changes in customer tastes and preferences, and offer rival incumbents and new entrants the opportunity of providing new and superior value enhancing goods and services based on competencies that the firm does not currently have.

In the medium to long term most, if not all, a firms' successful strategic formulae are challengeable: rivals will imitate success where they can, or devise alternative means of securing their differential advantage which may offer superior customer value. Patents or other forms of protection are not necessarily enduring since any high profits they endow will incentivise others to by-pass them in some way. The obvious conclusion is that the major secure means of obtaining a sustainable competitive advantage is to continue to invest in customer perceived innovations.

In essence, therefore, organisations should acknowledge that all strategic positions are contestable; that successful innovation will breed imitators; and that this in itself suggests that organisations need to direct attention to ensuring the speedy and extensive adoption of their innovations, while also developing the successor innovations, a juggling act that many organisations fail to perform.

Innovation

Innovation assumes many guises: it can involve the development of new technologically based products, such as DVD players; novel organisational processes, such as Easy Jet's approach to providing lower cost airline tickets; new forms of distribution through the expeditious use of the Internet; or different packaging, such as Tetra Pak. They can involve minor adjustments to, for example, existing technologies, or the development of products based on radically new technology. However whether or not one categorises a product such as Wrigley's 'Extra Thin Ice' mouth freshener, which consists of wafers of peppermint flavoured melt-in-the-mouth strips, as a radical or incremental innovation is unimportant. Nor will the consumer be engaged with categorising as a major or minor innovation the Unipath Clearblue Pregnancy Testing kit. Nor is the customer particularly interested in the science or technology underlying a new product. Rather the customer is concerned about what benefits the innovation offers. Similarly, the values of the innovative development as viewed by those involved with its development are irrelevant if they are not similarly perceived by the potential customer. Taking the stance of the potential customer is essential but it is a challenge to those who are committed to an innovation and who may therefore not always be sufficiently sensitive to intelligence that questions their faith in it.

Risks and uncertainties

We have stressed the advantages, indeed the necessity, of innovation (Rothwell et al. 1974). There is however a downside: the risk of failure is high. Extensive analysis of the causes of unsuccessful innovation have highlighted a number of primary reasons: a focus on the product idea rather than on what customers actually want; a failure to invest sufficiently in all aspects of marketing, such as service support; prolonged development from inadequate organisational communications; frequent changes in product specification during the development; inadequate resource provision at the outset and generally poor planning that results in a loss of market advantage to others; ineffective cost control; a rejection of external sources in favour of retaining internal control even though they may provide a more speedy and effective solution to technical and other problems during the development; and the marketing of flawed innovations that inevitably generate adverse publicity, from which it can be costly and difficult to recover, and discontent among intermediaries and customers.

A number of generic prescriptions have been suggested (Rothwell et al. 1974, Cooper 1979):

- Focus on identifying customer requirements
- Develop an effective marketing strategy that pays attention to communicating the benefits of the innovation and provides both wholesaler/retailer and customer support, including training, technical advice, instructions on use
- Ensure that there is effective internal communications between all those actors involved in the development including research, development, design, manufacturing, distribution, finance and marketing
- Develop and capitalise on external knowledge networks that can provide information, which permits the rapid solution of technical problems, and intelligence on market and other developments
- Market innovations that have been thoroughly tested for technical robustness, possible adverse consequences for consumers etc.
- Make provision for ensuring the necessary resources are available when they are required
- Devise at the outset an innovation development programme with 'milestones' at which progress can be reviewed
- Ensure that there is a champion who is committed to the innovation and who has the authority to command resources, deal with

issues relating to the development and in general assume responsibility for progressing the innovation

Yet despite the extensive research on why innovations fail, the risks remain high. There may be at least two explanations: first there continues to be widespread ignorance of the reasons for failure and how to deal with them. Secondly, the effective implementation of at least some of these prescriptions remains problematic. Take the finding that 'successful innovators have identified customers' needs'. It is hardly insightful to argue that *ex post* analyses of profitable innovations have found them to be useful to those who purchase them! Studies of failed developments at the time they originated may also suggest that the developers believed there was a market need. For example, Du Pont saw there was potentially a dramatic future shortage of natural leather for footwear and that therefore there was a need for a synthetic substitute. Its expensive and structurally sophisticated solution, the 'poromeric' Corfam, was however a costly failure, while the cheaper, PVC-coated fabrics managed to secure a significant market share. The difficulty is in identifying the product specification that is likely to result in sufficient market demand.

Unfortunately the clear and precise definition of customer specifications at the early stage of a development is not straightforward: customers may not be able to articulate what they want at the beginning because they may think in generalities, for instance, 'leather', and in the light of their experiences; while their requirements may change over time, and may be modified by what is available such as, for example, 'PVC materials'. Even if the producer elicits a clear statement of customers' wants, customers may reject the producer's interpretation of them. Moreover customer intentions often differ markedly from their behaviour: even at the late state of a product development, favourable customer attitudes do not necessarily suggest that they will purchase the product. There are a multitude of contaminants that can affect the customer's reactions and these combined with the producer's disposition to interpret responses favourably can lead to misleading conclusions. There are also external changes in the economic, political or regulatory climate or developments by existing or new competitors that can all have an impact on the original assumptions on which the innovative development was based.

The mists of uncertainty surrounding the innovation are not so easily dispelled, and may fog a clear understanding of the eventual outcome until relatively late in the development. All of this points to the need for a constant monitoring of customers' opinions of the evolving development and for a continuing review of any changes in market conditions. Any implications for the acceptability of the innovation need to be assessed carefully with changes in product specification and marketing strategy being made as appropriate. There may even be the need to consider the termination of the project.

However there is often a reluctance to abandon a project to which often senior executives in the organisation have publicly declared a commitment. Indeed, the presence of a champion who has the authority to secure and mobilise resources often creates strong resistance to the abortion of the development. Innovation champions are seen as critical to the success of an innovation because of the discomfort engendered by innovation: they campaign for the innovation, overcome obstacles and facilitate access to the necessary resources. Unfortunately their often unwavering commitment and access to power that are seen as such advantages, can also lead to costly prolongation of innovations that ultimately fail. There can be the inability to acknowledge intelligence and other signals pointing to the need to at least reappraise the development. Instead of treating invested resources as sunk costs, there is often a tendency to strive to recover resources already consumed by allocating more in the hope of eventually making a return. This only leads to heightened barriers to exit because of the even greater pressure to recover what has been invested. Eventually the need for more resources becomes so large without there being any prospects of ever achieving a profitable outcome that dramatic action often needs to be taken by those who have little or no association with the project – but only after unnecessary costs have been incurred.

Excessive caution can hamper innovation: the first signs of difficulties encourage the conservatives to argue for premature termination. The complexity of many innovative developments requires careful handling and planning. Yet clearly there is a tension between providing on the one hand an organisational climate that minimises the obstacles to effective innovation; and on the other having checks to ensure that inadequate innovations do not enjoy unfettered access to resources. One solution is to articulate clearly the original basis on which the innovation is being considered, outline broadly how its development is expected to unfold, and identify those progression points at which the conscious allocation of significant resources will need to be made. There is much to be said for involving independent experience in the management of innovation and possibly knowledge-able in the markets at which the innovation is aimed when evaluating the implications of any changes on the marketability of the innovation and assessing the future yield from any further allocation of resources. This approach recognises the need for incremental commitments when faced with the uncertainties that inevitably accompany innovation.

Customer focused

The development of an innovation is a process of continual enlighten-ment, with the evolution of the innovation shaped by additional intel-ligence, such as new market information, external developments, such as actions taken by competitors, and the feedback from decisions already made, such as customer reactions to prototypes.

The source of the innovation may be creative speculation about what customers may want; the detailed analysis of trends, technological activity, competitors' activities, the longitudinal studies of customers' behaviour, some serendipitous discovery during the course of planned research and development activity, or simply a bright idea. The innova-tion may result from structured analysis of markets which highlight some potential gap, or from an organisation's desire to broaden its product portfolio. Whatever the origins, it is important to check that it resonates with potential customers. Thus to enter the block chocolate market where there are long entrenched major players could only be undertaken with confidence when extensive consumer research using in depth focus groups highlighted dissatisfaction with the existing products, leading to the development of a 'chunky' bar that offered the 'bitiness' and value for money not offered by existing products. The resulting product was a runaway success, but stimulated quick responses from established rivals. The science of monoclonal antibodies promised considerable advantages for over-the-counter diagnostic kits. The development of an easy to use pregnancy testing kit, founded on the science, was the product of careful research of the benefits sought by female consumers, the development of a product with observable differential advantages over the competition, the implementation of a sound marketing programme, and the rapid formation of an interna-tional distribution chain (Littler and Leverick 1994, pp. 203–4). Moreover, because of the probability of a likely aggressive response from the incumbents in the market the company embarked on the development of a second-generation product that offered considerable improvements even before the original product was launched. The product was a major success. The company demonstrated a detailed attention to customer values by thoroughly researching what they required from pregnancy diagnosis. This example clearly illustrates the vitally important role of marketing in translating complex science into a form palatable to the customer.

In general, the uncovering of customer requirements is far from the simple: it is likely to involve more than carrying out surveys that ask consumers to react to some product proposal or opinionate on what they would like. Customers will often find it difficult to visualise some possible future in which there may be an imaginary product; they are likely to present perspectives based on existing experiences; and they may not be conscious of whether or not they might respond positively to a possible innovation until actually presented with it. Reactions gathered from surveys or even from straightforward focus groups might deviate significantly from what customers will do when faced with the development. Extensive market research can often mislead. For example, General Electric in the USA used mock-ups of TVs with eight different screen sizes, weights and prices to gauge consumer reaction and found they placed a low price on television portability. They did not proceed with the development. Shortly afterwards, Sony successfully launched a high priced transistor micro TV (Rosenbloom and Abernathy 1982).

The key to successful innovative is likely to involve the adventurous use of a variety of different research approaches – ethnography, structured observation, in-depth discussions, experimentation, projective techniques, focus groups, diaries, as well as surveys. Multiple analyses of data using researchers acting independently will encourage dialogue and heighten the probability of generating interesting and useful insights. The use of prototypes, and the exploitation of developments in information technology to assess customer responses to different design possibilities and experiences, are all likely to enhance the marketer's understanding. Information garnered by different methods should be compared and contrasted and unexplained differences explored. Not only should the attitudes, desires, and requirements of customers be monitored throughout the development, for the reasons already explained, but also there should be longitudinal research on the changing aspirations and behaviour of any organisation's customers. Apart from highlighting changing attitudes towards the organisation and its offerings, it can assist in identifying the altering dynamics of customer behaviour. In some way marketers need to be able to employ this emerging conflicting, speculative and ambiguous information to develop an understanding of their customers and the customers' perceptions of the developing innovation.

Customer acceptance

There tends to be much emphasis on the development of the innovation, and yet its ultimate success is heavily dependent on how effectively information about it is disseminated, that is, on how the marketing of the innovation is effected. Customers have to be informed of the innovation's existence, to be persuaded of its values, and to have a positive experience in purchasing, installing, employing or consuming the innovation. Adopters are often themselves effective marketers because they communicate their experiences either verbally or by public display.

At the beginning of the new product development, research (Rogers 1983) suggests that marketers need to address at least five questions:

First, what are the perceived advantages of the innovation: does it offer additional benefits over existing ways of meeting customer requirements or does it offer significantly new values?

Second, does the innovation require changes in customer behaviour? If it does are the perceived advantages such as to outweigh the costs involved in any changes – retraining, learning new ways of doing things, investing in new equipment?

Third, is the innovation simple to understand and use?

Fourth, are the benefits of the innovation demonstrable? For example, will non-users be able to observe the advantages of the innovation?

Fifth, will it be possible to try out the innovation at little if any cost so that the risks associated with any change are minimised?

There is a clear correlation between positive responses to each of these questions and the acceptability of the innovation. And speed of acceptance is generally of the essence: if the new product is seen as successful, and more especially if it adversely affects competitors, then the innovator will only have a limited time to capitalise on its lead before its rivals respond with imitative or even innovative alternatives; the early captured consumers can form an established long term source of demand, particularly if there are significant switching costs; while significant early market penetration results in speedy payback and profits.

Generating rapid and widespread awareness can be achieved by all of the traditional methods – advertising, promotion, public relations, personal selling, and even here creativity can have an important role.

But it is obvious that interpersonal communication between those who are aware of the innovation, and may have adopted it, and others can also be an influential means of spreading both awareness and knowledge.

It has been suggested that there may be major players in the word-of-mouth process called opinion leaders (Littler 2001), who may be seen as credible sources of, or who may be active in, spreading information about an innovation. Therefore, it would appear that the cost effectiveness of the communications would be enhanced by targeting communications at these individuals who would then assume a major role in disseminating information about the innovation. This strategy however may not be so easily realised. There are no media that have opinion leaders as an exclusive or semi exclusive audience. Rather opinion leaders are likely to be members of the mass audience. Moreover, opinion leaders are not controllable: they cannot be directed to convey positive messages about the innovation, indeed they may act to dissuade rather than persuade. There may not be generic opinion leadership, just as there is unlikely to be generic innovativeness: both probably vary with product categories. Opinion leadership which itself may be connected with innovativeness, that is the extent to which people have a disposition to adopt an innovation before others, may be related to, for example, people's leisure interests or professional activities. In a sense all potential customers are opinion leaders in that all those who are likely buyers may be sufficiently interested in the innovation both to seek information and communicate information about it.

The overriding goal therefore is to ensure that knowledge of the innovation is rapidly disseminated among the potential customers for the innovation and that interest in it can be satisfied through widespread availability of the innovation.

Summary

I have noted the importance of ensuring that organisations have the momentum of continuous innovation because the notion of a sustainable competitive advantage is contentious: all positions are contestable in the medium to long term. Organisations therefore need to have a clear strategy of innovation, and plans for constant product improvement in line with changing customer values. They should identify sources of complacency and resistance to innovation and have in place means of overcoming them. I have also noted that having an early significant market penetration for any innovation is heavily dependent on the rapid dissemination of information about the innovation: without that it is obvious that diffusion will be impeded.

References

Bacon, Francis (1625) 'Of Innovations' in *Essays*. Accessed via: *http://ourworld. compuserve.com/homepage/mike_donnally/lotFIVE.htm*

Barney, J. (1991) 'Firm Resources and Sustained Competitive Advantage', *Journal of Management*, Vol. 17, No. 1, pp. 99–120.

Cooper, R.G. (1979) 'The dimensions of industrial new product success and failure', *Journal of Marketing*, Vol. 43, No. 1 (Summer) pp. 93–103.

Economist, The (2003) 'Screen Test – Is Reuters Seriously Ill?' February 20th 2003.

Hall, R. (1992) 'The Strategic Analysis of Intangible Resources', *Strategic Management Journal*, Vol. 13, No. 2, pp. 135–144.

Littler, D. and Leverick, F. (1994) 'Competitiveness in new technology sectors' in Saunders, J. (ed.) *The Marketing Initiative*, London: Prentice Hall, pp. 186–205.

Littler, D. (2001) 'The Idiosyncracies of New Product Adoption for Technologically Innovative Offerings', *The Marketing Review*, Vol. 2, No. 1, pp. 3–19.

Rothwell, R., Freeman, ?. Horsley, A., Jervis, V.T.P., Robertson, A.B. and Townsend, J. (1974) 'SAPPHO updated – project SAPPHO phase II', *Research Policy*, Vol. 3, No. 3, pp. 258–91.

Rogers, E.M. (1983) *The Diffusion of Innovations*, New York: Free Press.

Rosenbloom, R.S. and Abernathy, W.J. (1982) 'The Climate for Innovation in Industry: The Role of Management Attitudes and Practices in Consumer Electronics', *Research Policy*, Vol. 11, No. 4, pp. 209–225.

Schumpeter, J.A. (1950) Capitalism, *Socialism and Democracy* 3rd edition, New York: Harper.

Shah, S. (2003) 'Reuters Hopes New Products Will Help Recapture Past Glory', *The Independent*, 30th April, p. 20.

5

Invisible Forces: How Consumer Interactions Make the Difference

Jacob Goldenberg *

Introduction

Several years ago, an email containing the following attachment was sent to numerous recipients at the Hebrew University Business School:

> don't open a PPS file named : PALESTINE !!!!!!!
> it contains a virus that will erase your hard disk !!!!!!!
> E R A S E I T ! ! ! ! !!!!!!!
> (even from the deleted items)
> pass it on!

Obedient recipients discovered that in forwarding the email, they were in fact spreading a computer virus, planted – with a warped sense of humour – inside a virus warning. This virus, fortunately of the benign variety, was a harbinger of what has since become a pervasive internet phenomenon, one that has been enthusiastically adopted by the marketing community in the form of 'viral marketing'.

Viral marketing is a recent buzz word, a concept which has spread in a manner similar to the epidemiological process it imitates. This approach likens products, ideas or even the relationships that organisations establish with their customers, to viruses which multiply and spread through interactions. Just as a virus spreads through infection, products are conceptualised to 'infect' those individuals with whom

* Acknowledgement: I acknowledge the opportunity of working with colleagues, Barak Libai and Eitan Muller. This essay is grounded in our work. For more details about joint research projects please access: complexmarkets.com

they come into contact. This 'system of infection' is obviously beneficial to marketers, who conserve their own resources by utilising their exponentially increasing number of customers to perform marketing activities instead.

Our current understanding of the market as a complex system amenable to such efficient manipulations is still limited. Recognizing the complexity and self-organisation of marketing systems will lead to new conceptualisations of markets as adaptive systems that manifest extremely strong forces. New insights into this significant process may be incorporated in marketing practice with the aim of reducing the failure rate of new products and accelerating product adoption processes.

Invisible forces

Much of the knowledge on the adoption of new products in the market accumulated over recent decades is of a practical, instructive nature. One such accepted truism in marketing, supported by PDMA (*Product Development Management & Association*) survey findings (See PDMA handbook of new product development; Rosenau et al. 1996), is that a new product, which offers a solution to a problem, has a greater chance of success than one which offers a superior marketing mix, yet resolves no problem. However, the rate of new product failures is distressingly high (Goldenberg et al. 2001a), even discounting innovations which fail to provide for a genuine consumer need. When we consider the cumulative wealth of marketing experience available to manufacturers and marketers of new products, this fact alone is sufficient to undermine confidence in marketing savvy. The obvious question is; what are marketers doing wrong?

Actually, I believe that we are making fairly sophisticated use of the knowledge we have – it is the knowledge that we have *yet to acquire* that is working against our best efforts at new product development. New findings on how consumers communicate marketing information to each other may yield a wealth of valuable information for marketing professionals hoping to gain acceptance for new innovations they introduce to the market. The role of *Word of Mouth* (w-o-m hereafter) is far from a new concept: its significance in the adoption of new products has been recognised for several decades. Fortunately, scientific developments now provide the tools to investigate the phenomenon of word-of-mouth – the inherent complexity of the factors involved, as well as the changes in their relative significance. This elusive, yet fascinating marketing factor may hold the key to understanding the new product development process and, more specifically, why so many new products fail.

We can trace the concept of w-o-m to several sources, including the classic formulation of the product growth curve. This model of economic growth, embraced with enthusiasm by theoreticians and marketers alike, is based on the work of the economist and demographer Thomas Robert Malthus, who formulated the first equation describing the dynamics of auto-catalytically proliferating[1] individuals in 1798. A correction to Malthus' equation, offered by P.F. Verhuulst in 1838, ensured a more realistic growth pattern with saturation terms. The Verhuulst logistic equation is almost identical to the models we use today in marketing.

In the field of marketing, this basic notion was taken up by two researchers who established a broad framework for insights into the adoption of innovations. In 1962, Everett Rogers published the first edition of his book 'Diffusion of Innovation'. Through case study analysis, Rogers uncovered the fundamental sociological structure describing how adopters of new products interact with each other, influence each other's adoption and rejection decisions, ultimately affecting the diffusion of innovations in a market. Several years later, Frank Bass (1969) developed a quantitative model of diffusion, based on a model taken from the field of epidemiology. In this model, consumers are either infected spontaneously (i.e., adopt the new product) or through contact with other consumers (previous purchasers of the product). Extending this biological analogy, Rogers established the critical role of interpersonal contact in the diffusion of new products as one of the most basic assumptions of his model. He assumed, for example, that infection through contact is greater than spontaneous infection (as represented by effects such as advertising and marketing efforts).

Together, the premises of Bass and Rogers provided the foundation for the concept of the product growth curve (visually similar to the product life cycle and also known as the adoption curve or the diffusion curve). The product growth curve represents the introduction of an innovation into a market as a progression along a successful path, in which early adopters generate subsequent product acceptance by the main market. They do this by virtue of their basic attributes and social roles, bolstered by a host of marketing activities, including advertising. Indeed, innovators and early adopters are conceptualised based on their unique contribution to other population groups in the form of product-related information. The information that early adopters convey – either in the form of data injected into the market by marketers and actively sought or passively received by consumers; or as information passed directly or indirectly from one consumer to another – reduces uncertainty in subsequent consumer decision making. In addition to their ability to reduce the perceived risks associated with an innovation by communicating product-related information, early adopters also instigate a process of social emulation and provide the basis for social legitimisation.

The original model, appealing in its simplicity, admittedly captured a truth, but as theories mature and our environment undergoes rapid changes, growing evidence also points to significant deviations from the model. In fact, in as many as 50 per cent of all new products, the shape of the resulting diffusion curve significantly deviates from the classic model. It has become increasingly obvious that the growth of contemporary markets and products is driven by a host of intricately interwoven factors, which the classic adoption curve fails to reflect, and therefore fails to predict.

As marketers, we know the amount invested in advertising, the number of coupons distributed, the number of sales promotion personnel hired and so forth. We are able to measure the inputs and outputs of various elements comprising our distribution channel and even assess the long-term contribution of each. However, since we lack understanding of the weight consumers attribute to information, recommendations or warnings they receive from friends and acquaintances in their purchase decisions, the effect of w-o-m tends to catch us unprepared. Emmanuel Rosen (2000) presents some surprising data confirming the strong impact of word-of-mouth on sales. For example, 65 per cent of all PDA (Personal Digital Assistant) purchasers reported learning about their hand-held organiser from their friends and 70 per cent of all Americans select their physician based on personal recommendations. It is not surprising that the implications of this factor have remained unnoticed for so long. The unique feature of *word of mouth* (w-o-m) is the almost surreptitious nature of the process it generates beneath the surface of the market and marketing data: it is a factor which is visible only when its ultimate results become accessible for analysis, in the form of the sales data. The process of transmitting and communicating information from individual to individual and the manner in which individual consumers are differentially affected remain a mystery to market researchers.

One of the causes of this gap in knowledge is the underlying complexity of the w-o-m process. The way in which information spreads in a given social system may be described as 'an adaptive complex system', i.e., a system that consists of a large number of individual entities which interact with each other (in a manner that is sometimes indiscernible), ultimately generating large-scale, collective (macro), visible behaviour (Waldorp 1992). Although in many such adaptive systems the interactions themselves may be simple, the magnitude of the system's scale admits the emergence of patterns which are hard to predict, hard to track empirically and often almost impossible to analyse analytically. Fortunately, recent computer applications offer a more methodical and comprehensive approach to capturing, tracking and measuring these 'off-stage' interpersonal interactions, specifically with regard to the factors which affect these communications.

Enter Cellular Automata – a computer simulation model that allows us to peek behind the scenes, so to speak, and expose the micro-processes underlying the aggregate end result of sales data. This sophisticated, yet simple, technique drills down market analysis to the level of the individual in the social network and therefore more closely approximates the operation of w-o-m in practice than previous adoption models, which track aggregate market results and thus remain 'on the surface'. For more details, and to experience this environment through an excel demonstration see *www.complexmarkets.com*.

Cellular Automata depicts the adoption process as a time-dependent adaptation/change of a social network, based on interpersonal communication parameters, rather than a market development curve based on sales data.

The fact that the destiny of a new product may be decided by the nature of the relationship between individual consumers may make many marketing managers queasy. How, in practice, can marketing managers seek to influence the underlying social structure of society? Although they may intuitively feel that they have little control over this process, new insights reveal that managers today have more control than they believe. However, they must be alert to the fact that mistaken interpretation of the w-o-m process can easily lead to misguided and expensive marketing decisions. For these, there is no tolerance in our highly competitive world.

The saddle phenomenon: a case of word-of-mouth driven markets

One illustration of the significant role of word-of-mouth in the adoption process is offered in a recent extension of the classic adoption curve – the Dual Market phenomenon, purporting to reflect a more accurate representation of new product development by attributing the high failure rate of new products to communications between individual consumers (or the lack thereof). The model, also known as Moore's Chasm Theory (Moore 1991), is supported by a wealth of anecdotal evidence. Among other examples Moore describes how the Palm Pilot successfully crossed a marketing chasm (the term chasm is explained shortly) to become a successful product, while previous products and model were able to penetrate only unique type of consumers (e.g. the innovators), but failed to spark the interest of the rest of the market.

Ascribing a large number of new product failures to the marketers' disregard of an important twist on the classic adoption theory, Moore cautions marketers to recognise that the adoption of a new product critically depends on its reception in *two* distinct markets. Rather than a single, general market in which consumers may be differentiated according to their 'adopter category', these two markets form as a direct result of the inherent communication barrier that exists between early adopters and the main market.

Moore claims that due to this discontinuity in communications between early adopters and the 'main market', that is, the majority of consumers, early adopters fail to function as a source of information for purchase decisions by the remainder of the market. The potential for marketing failure can be minimised if marketers realise that w-o-m communication between the two types of consumers is sufficiently rich and extensive; or when the product or element of the marketing mix is changed to address the main market needs (that are different from the early market). In some cases, a price chance can signal a desire to attract the next layer of price sensitive customers.

This intuitively appealing idea has been confirmed by empirical evidence in Goldenberg et al. (2002). While the chasm refers to communication between two sub-markets, it is important to look at sales data and see whether the chasm is just another factor of failure or is it an immanent mechanism. Indeed, when the sales data for innovative products were tracked over time, it was clear that new product adoption takes place in two semi-consecutive loci – two different consumer markets, with distinct consumer attributes. Specifically, using an information bank containing data on a large number of innovative products in the consumer electronics industry, we found that approximately one-third of the cases involved a pattern consisting of an initial peak, giving rise to a trough of sufficient depth and duration to preclude random fluctuations, followed by sales which eventually exceeded the initial peak – a pattern which is termed a 'saddle'. When the inherent differences in the reception of new products by these two markets are sufficiently large, a lag occurs between the adoption patterns of the early market and the main market, creating two distinct sales peaks, rather than the single, classic Bass diffusion pattern.

Figure 5.1 is a graphic illustration of the relation of the dual-market to the saddle phenomenon, while Figure 5.2 presents a real case of the PC sales for consumers.

Moreover, using a microscopic representation tool that supports a computer simulation of the dual-market phenomenon, and definitions of several basic parameters (both markets begin at the same point in time and, although not isolated from each other, each has distinct market attributes and potential); it was possible to gain insight into the basic circumstances supporting the emergence of a saddle.

From a managerial point of view, this phenomenon warrants attention because a significant and unexpected decline in sales in the relatively early stages of a product's life cycle may erroneously cast doubt on product viability. Thus, identifying the conditions underlying the occurrence of a saddle may prevent premature withdrawal of new products. This is especially true for high-tech and similar innovative products, since firms typically continue R&D and product improvements after market launch, increasing their vulnerability to early sales fluctuations. Evidence of a decline in sales leads to a sudden, unexpected drop in the cash flow, just when firms are in the investment-intensive

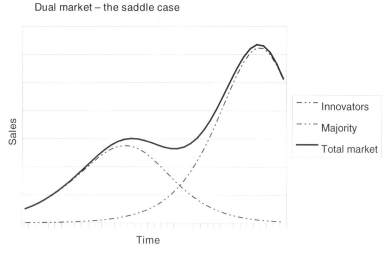

Figure 5.1   The saddle mechanism

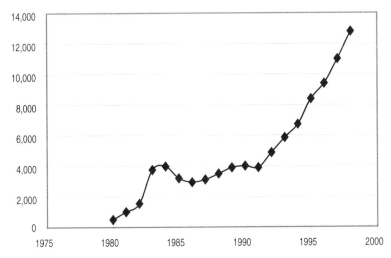

Figure 5.2 Saddle in personal computers

situation of simultaneously launching and improving the new product. The saddle's contribution in informing managerial decision-making at such a crucial stage in the introduction of a new product onto the market increases if we take into account that saddles may be even more ubiquitous than our statistics show. Using only data on products that ultimately survived the drop in sales and endured, we found evidence of a saddle in approximately one third of the products that were modeled. It would not be far-fetched to assume that, given the chance, many products that were 'killed' by managers faced with a drop in sales might have developed a subsequent sales peak.

Despite ostensible problems generated by a misleading saddle, several advantages embodied in the dual-market phenomenon work against efforts to eliminate the early market entirely and generate a later takeoff. This argument implies that a saddle might be a *necessary* stage for the successful introduction of an innovative product, enabling simultaneous introduction and improvement. First, transferring responsibility for product adoption and takeoff to the main market is an expensive decision and manipulation of the more hesitant main market adopters can be expected to be far more costly than investing in the early market. Second, by 'listening to their voice', firms leverage feedback from the early market as important input for further R&D and product improvements. By reducing or eliminating the early market, firms would lose a critical source of information.

Therefore, firms may prefer to optimise rather than eliminate, manipulating saddle size and timing by allocating resources and deciding on appropriate marketing strategies based on the saddle's predicted appearance.

The combination of these anecdotal and empirical findings highlights the important marketing opportunity for the introduction of new products that are offered by unique *potential* patterns of communications among the early market and the main market. Our study identified several parameters, which marketers can manipulate to affect some degree of control over saddle size (see Goldenberg et al. 2002), and experiencing the saddle dynamics in a simulation environment is offered in *complexmarkets.com*.

The most important parameters (which are also difficult to control) include the communication level between the two segments of the dual market (early and main market). Other parameters are the communication levels within each segment, and the marketing efforts (again within each segment). The last two are relatively easy to control however their impact on the shape of the entire adoption curve is less dramatic. Nevertheless, it is still important to effectively allocate marketing resources. For example, when the market of early adopters is in takeoff, it was found that it is almost pointless to invest more efforts in this type of consumer and it is advisable to transfer the resources to the mainstream market.

Advertising versus word of mouth

Cellular Automata and microscopic simulation tools allow us to construct and test market models based on theories and empirical data relating to the nature of social networks and inter-personal communications. One such theory, 'the strength of weak ties' (Granovetter 1973), proposes one of the most important conceptual explanations of the process by which micro-level interactions affect macro-level phenomena. Granovetter claimed that individuals are often influenced by others with whom they maintain tenuous or even random relationships. These influences are labelled 'weak ties', to distinguish them from the more stable, frequent and intimate 'strong tie' interactions that characterise an individual's personal network. Although weaker in absolute impact on the individual level, weak ties offer individuals access to external influences (individuals in distant networks). By creating connections between different groups, weak ties facilitate the spread of information throughout society. In fact, in the complete absence of weak ties, a given social system would subsequently consist exclusively of discrete and isolated personal networks.

Supporting Granovetter's hypothesis, Brown and Reingen (1987) found that although strong ties were perceived as influential in consumer decisions, weak ties were more likely to facilitate w-o-m referral flows, by providing access to extra-group opportunities and information. The idea was further developed in the recent bestseller 'The Tipping Point', by Malcolm Gladwell (2000). By identifying three groups of individuals, whom he calls 'mavens', 'connectors' and 'salesmen', each of whom plays a unique marketing role in connecting distinct groups, Gladwell illustrates how their involvement ignites the w-o-m process, which sweeps through society as fiercely as an epidemic.

Cellular Automata was also employed to test similar propositions (Goldenberg et al. 2001b). In this study, communications between different population groups were modelled by comparing the effects of 'strong' (in-group) and 'weak' (inter-group) ties among community members with the effects of advertising. The models tracked the spread of information in a society, based on the 'rules of dissemination' and the manipulation of a broad range of parameters (including social network size and the frequency of random interactions in the society). The study's findings empirically confirmed that w-o-m is a salient and significant factor driving all stages of the diffusion process. In fact, the influence of weak ties was found to be at least as strong as the influence of strong ties in causing the spread of w-o-m. Moreover, findings showed that both types of ties played a more significant role than advertising in informing consumer adoption decisions. Specifically, it was found that beyond a relatively early stage of the process, the efficacy of external marketing efforts diminishes and strong and weak ties become the main force propelling the adoption process.

Should we be surprised to find that consumers are more influenced in their adoption decisions by other consumers, in either proximal or remote social networks, than by information they receive from advertisers or manufacturers? Probably not. W-o-m fills this special position by helping consumers make sense of an over-abundance of product-related information in the environment. Rosen (2000) notes three possible reasons for the superiority of the w-o-m effect over advertising. First, as a result of the proliferation of advertisements, promotions, information and competition, consumers are no longer able to adequately attend to the voice of the advertiser. Second, today's consumers are increasingly suspicious and skeptical of advertising exaggerations and of advertisements as an objective source of information. Third, heightened interconnectivity among individuals today facilitates real time consultation and information sharing among members of personal networks.

One important managerial implication of these insights is that a significant proportion of a new product's budget – invested in advertising – may warrant strategic re-allocation. These empirical findings may serve as a warning sign to marketers to avoid exclusive or massive reliance on marketing media and rather direct their efforts towards affecting the w-o-m process occurring beneath the surface. Moreover, managers attempting to influence w-o-m spread are justified in distinguishing between the two types of social interactions which contribute to w-o-m communications (both positive and negative). For example, in certain situations managers may wish to differentiate between rewards for the referral of close friends and family members and rewards for referring others. Our study found that when personal networks are large, when random contacts among inter-network individuals are few, or when the advertising effect is strong, fostering inter-network ties may be one of the few options available to marketers.

The self-propagating product

To harness the potential power of w-o-m as a critical element in the dissemination of products requires an entire change of perspective in the new product development process. Instead of creating marketing *messages* designed to influence the individual, marketers should design their *products and communications* with an eye on their potential effect on w-o-m.

'Viral marketing' appears to be an extreme example of how managers attempt to exploit the very structure of social relations, by manipulating the frequency and intensity of product-related interactions. Typically, 'viral marketing' is erroneously understood to encompass any marketing process in which the consumers themselves function as sales promoters. Yet viral marketing is more than triggering positive product recommendations to generate and increase sales. Advertising campaigns that encourages viewers or listeners to talk to others about the product, or promotion efforts aimed at building a strong brand name are illustrations of legitimate marketing activities that, if applied skillfully and appropriately, facilitate the achievement of marketing objectives. They are not, however, examples of viral marketing. In genuine viral marketing, a situation is created in which consumers who have already adopted a new product are *personally motivated* to be proactive in spreading positive w-o-m and recruit increasingly more new adopters, even to the extent of active persuasion efforts.

The introduction of the facsimile machine is an excellent example. After an extremely lengthy introduction period extending over 20 years, the sales curve of the fax reflects an extremely steep slope, suggesting a shift to massive adoption in a short period. This exceptionally steep takeoff curve (see Figure 5.3) disguises a process occurring beneath the surface of the market, which left no mark on the product's sales curve over this 20-year period.

This 'unexpected' sales success can be traced to a very interesting characteristic of the fax machine: the benefits accruing to each fax consumer increase as a positive function of the total number of fax-users in his or her social (or business) network. Driven by their own desire to maximise their benefits from their purchase, fax-owning individuals are motivated to expand the potential usage network by 'spreading the word', inducing others to adopt the new technology. The extended introduction phase, followed by a steep rise in the sales curve of fax machines, reflects the gradual accretion of a sufficiently large mass of fax adopters who put pressure to bear on the mass market to adopt the new innovation. In viral marketing, consumer motivation is harnessed to attain a similar critical mass, which generates the seemingly magical

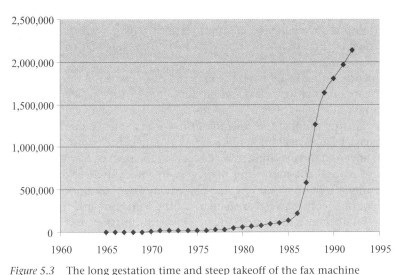

Figure 5.3 The long gestation time and steep takeoff of the fax machine

stage of 'takeoff', a necessary condition for product success. At that point, late adopters are virtually 'impelled' to purchase the innovation, if only to maintain their previous status in the system. If a business decides to forgo the purchase of a fax machine, it soon finds itself 'out of the loop', unable to conduct business with its suppliers and customers.

Email itself is another excellent example of how a user's own motivation generates sufficient pressure to induce others to adopt a new technology. Software companies also employ a viral model of marketing when they offer frequent new versions and product updates: most consumers purchase new versions simply to ensure compatibility of communications with earlier adopters. The fax is a classical case of product externality, but viral marketing may be applied even without such a trait. Other, perhaps less imaginative examples are sales promotion campaigns for membership clubs, which give credits to members who refer other potential members. Consumers, unwittingly manipulated by marketers, can engage in word-of-mouth action driven by the understanding that, the greater the number of adopters, the more each individual benefits from the innovation.

Although many Internet products such as ICQ (short for 'I Seek You')[2] spread virally, the Internet itself is not a sufficient condition for viral marketing: although the Internet offers an advantage by facilitating interactive communication among consumers, the WWW is merely the medium of communication. Marketers have the far-from-simple task of providing a motive capable of initiating and sustaining inter-personal communications. The pivotal question for marketers then becomes, how can w-o-m be triggered to spread in viral form?

Incorporating insights on the material role of word-of-mouth in the dissemination of new ideas and products may be the first step in developing a new type of marketing model, which we may call 'the self-propagating product.' As research into w-o-m expands, marketers will perhaps be able to employ this model to harness the enormous potential of w-o-m in launching new products to the market. Since it may be more natural for marketing managers to direct their efforts to the manipulation of marketing factors which have traditionally been under their control, such as elements of the marketing mix, potentially fruitful directions of research include investigating the effect of manipulating various product traits on the spread of w-o-m. Further research may confirm whether such manipulations ultimately ignite, boost and sustain sales. Still, a word of caution is warranted.

On the dangers of metaphors

A word of caution is warranted. The concept of 'viral marketing' is also an example of how marketing, as a field, engenders countless metaphors that attempt or appear to transform marketing into a simple practice. Marketing as a 'battlefield' for example, is one metaphor which has ignited the enthusiasm of many managers: managers 'move troops', 'inflict casualties on their competitors', employ tactics of 'guerrilla warfare' and 'recover from their defeats'. Similarly, well-documented is the use of biological metaphors to represent elements and phenomena in the new product dissemination process, based on the similarity between the propagation of ideas in society and the reproduction of organisms. In his 1956 study of science and morality, Sperry noted the similarity between regeneration processes and evolutionary processes. Jacques Monod (1971), a molecular biologist, subsequently expanded this insight and claimed that even ideas have some of the attributes of living organisms: just as organisms reproduce and compete for the environmental resources they need in order to propagate, human minds contain only a limited quantity of resources that must be allocated to develop and reproduce ideas. The famous biologist, Richard Dawkins (1990), proposed a dynamic for the spread of abstract ideas and social and cultural perceptions (which he called 'memes') and the subsequent 'infection' of other individuals.

The use of metaphors undisputedly facilitates the cognitive comprehension of ideas. Especially in the form of '10 Steps to a Successful Marketing Launch' or similar, metaphors are highly seductive and are assimilated without really examining whether these prescriptions genuinely offer a clear and sufficiently productive thesis to guide practice. The ostensibly simplistic solutions implied by metaphors tend to deaden our sense of critical perception and their appeal is enhanced by biased statistics. Confirming evidence generally lacks information on those cases in which implementation was either impossible, led to ineffective results or was rejected after deliberation, or cases in which the implementation of the easy-to-follow steps led to a marketing failure. The seemingly refreshing, light-hearted nature of metaphors also creates a climate where managers feel professionally obligated to 'update their toolbox' with increasing frequency, in tune with newly emerging metaphors.

To attain sound knowledge, however, the application of science is essential in distinguishing slogans from genuine insights and conducting rigorous knowledge-generating investigations. Receptiveness to the lessons of the word of mouth process requires marketers to consciously avoid the indiscriminate application of simplistic slogans and rules, and recognise that no short cuts exist.

Harnessing hidden resources – the potential for creativity

In the systematic search for untapped insights and resources, science provides the rigor of research, the ability to delve deeply into hidden processes, such as word-of-mouth. Marketing, however, does not rely solely on science: it is considered to be the meeting point of science and art. Art provides marketing with the wings to soar, unhampered by existing conceptions or conventional reasoning. Indeed, to enhance our knowledge in the future requires not only a wise combination of both perspectives, but an understanding of the relationship between the three fields of science, marketing and art, as points on a continuum of creativity. Art, as the realm of original thought and creative ideas, has much to teach marketing professionals and it is perhaps not surprising that even in the field of creativity, science holds the promise for uncovering its lessons.

While each discipline makes a vital contribution to marketing practice, both exert powerful, but opposite pressures on problem-solving in marketing. This is especially noticeable in New Product Development, a field where creativity and originality are an important factor, and yet the inherent differences between science and art have translated into a traditional separation and rivalry between marketing and engineering in the NPD process. From an engineering viewpoint, science is used in new product development specifically to increase usefulness and efficiency. While the contribution of original scientific reasoning is recognised in science, originality does not serve as a criterion for choosing which of a variety of ideas to adopt. Scientific problem-solving involves the application of predefined, precise standards to reduce the range of possible solutions to a limited number of 'correct solutions'. Indeed, the inherent value of scientific theory lies in its being 'correct'. On the other hand, marketing a creative idea is valued in its own right, in combination with other values such as quality, efficiency, and reliability. Originality, surprise and innovation are part of the creative mix aspired to and produced by marketing organisations and a marketing solution is frequently judged by virtue of its creativity rather than its conformity to a set of pre-defined rules. Nevertheless, when product development lies exclusively in the hands of designers, originality generally comes at the expense of considerations of functionality, effectiveness and/or efficiency.

For creative ideas to be successfully received by the market, both types of input are needed: the knowledge of science to provide inputs of feasibility and effectiveness; and creative intuition and talent to achieve the measure of innovation necessary to attract the attention of the market.

True, in many companies, the long-standing rivalry between marketing and engineering has been replaced by an organisational climate which seeks to foster collaboration and cooperation between both domains, by involving design professionals in the early stages of new product development. Still, the tension that remains between the corporate representatives of these two bodies of knowledge is a sign that a different solution may be warranted. Recent voices have called for a hybrid 'innovation manager' in NPD – an expert with sufficient knowledge in both engineering and marketing, able to understand the technological aspects of the products no less than the taste of its potential consumers. Yet even a formal merger of science, creative design and marketing may be insufficient, as it is becoming increasingly clear that this new specialisation also requires in-depth 'archeological' knowledge of innovations. This is especially highlighted by the high rate of new product failures and the high percentage of R&D budgets allocated to NPD, most of this directed to the introduction stage.

Future organisations may be expected to employ NPD professionals who offer a combination of marketing skills and expertise in creativity and innovations (including archeological knowledge of product development, such as anecdotal evidence and cumulative experience, theoretical and practical knowledge of quantitative models, and the research ability to reveal underlying trends), as well as engineering know-how and understanding of science and technology.

The central role of new product development in organisations, coupled with the significance of creativity in marketing, opens up current thinking and research to new ideas about the human potential with regard to creativity training. Traditionally, researchers held that the creative thinking process is qualitatively different from 'ordinary' day-to-day thinking, involving a leap which cannot be scientifically formulated, analysed or reconstructed. It is therefore not surprising that no thorough scientific investigation of creativity was conducted until recent decades.

In the past 30 years, numerous methods for fostering creativity have appeared and spread. Common to all these methods is the concept that in order to ignite the 'creative spark', we merely need to disassociate from existing thought frameworks and search diligently for the non-conventional, suspending judgment and criticism. Despite the growing popularity of various creativity enhancement methods, a significant shift has occurred from the mystical perception of creativity which describes the creative process as 'an expression of a divine spark' to a more scientifically oriented approach to the process.

As academic research began to confirm or deny beliefs, feelings and assumptions connected with creative thinking, a scientific knowledge base in this area emerged. The pioneers in breaking the 'academic taboo' on research in this field were cognitive psychologists, later joined by investigators in other disciplines such as neuro-psychology, Artificial Intelligence, engineering, education, and, more recently, marketing and management science.

A relatively recent development in this field of research is the growing use of computers to test explicit models of creative processes. Computerised approaches to creativity are based on the concept that individual creative thought can be translated into a computer program with the aid of artificial intelligence (AI) techniques (Mayer 1999). The conceptualisation of creativity as mental calculation stems from a cognitive approach which focuses on individual capabilities of reasoning and knowledge as the basis for creative work. This claim is supported in a number of scientific fields, including research on problem-solving in engineering (Altshuler 1986), advertising and New Product Development (Goldenberg, Mazursky and Solomon 1999a, b, c). Although not without shortcomings, the strength of the computerised approach is in the precision it brings to creativity research and its offer of a method to enhance individual creativity in a systematic manner.

Technological developments and originality are combined in one such effort to systemise training in creativity. The *Creative Templates* method (Goldenberg and Mazursky 2002), currently used to teach marketing professionals engaged in NPD, was developed through a joint effort on the part of advertising and marketing professionals and scientists, a collaboration which is undoubtedly a major factor behind its strength. In guiding professionals to solve problems creatively, this method involves the identification of a unique way of solving a well-known problem, or alternatively, the identification of an important, yet unnoticed problem. Studies have unequivocally indicated that template training generates some improvement in individual creativity, pointing to the possibility of enhancing the quality of marketing solutions through training in ideation and creativity.

The implication of these studies is that creativity is amenable to the application of scientific tools and professional training. Recent insights into the human potential for developing creativity thus open up entirely new vistas for human endeavour in the field of innovations and NPD, and will hopefully enhance the effectiveness efforts to provide consumers with an ever-new array of new products which satisfies the infinite bundle of human needs with greater-than-ever success.

Afterword

Consumer interactions constitute one, albeit fascinating, of many processes working beneath the surface to ultimately find expression as marketing effects. With the help of recent advances in research and technologies, we now have keys to uncover facets of the powerful yet invisible forces operating beneath the surface of the market. As our awareness of the complexity of our world grows, recent developments in contemporary society drive the formation of a new structure in which these forces play an increasingly significant and compelling role. Much remains to be discussed and even more remains to be discovered. Our task is made difficult by the fact that, as a field, marketing still lacks a tradition for attending to, tracking, charting and analysing invisible data of this kind. Nevertheless, given the evidence for the strength of these forces and their intriguing effect on the destiny of new products, our efforts in this direction are warranted. This is where marketing should direct its efforts in the next decade.

References

Altschuller, G.S. (1986) *To find an idea: Introduction to the theory of solving problems of Inventions*, Novosibirsk, USSR, Nauka.

Bass, Frank M. (1969) A New Product Growth Model for Consumer Durables, *Management Science*, Vol. 15, 1 (January), pp. 215–27.

Johnson-Brown, J. and Reingen, P.H. (1987) Social Ties and Word-of-Mouth Referral Behavior, *Journal of Consumer Research* 14, 3 (December), 350–362.

Dawkins, R. (1990) *The Selfish Gene*, Oxford University Press, England.

Gladwell, M. (2000) *The Tipping Point*, Back Bay books, Boston.

Goldenberg, J., Mazursky, D. and Solomon, S. (1999a) Templates of original innovation: Projecting original incremental innovations from intrinsic information, *Technological Forecasting and Social Change,* May, Vol. 61/1, 1–12.

Goldenberg, J., Mazursky, D. and Solomon, S. (1999b): Creative Sparks, *Science*, Vol. 285, (5433) September 1495–6.

Goldenberg, J., Mazursky, D. and Solomon, S. (1999c): Toward Identifying the Inventive Templates of New Products: A Channeled Ideation Approach, *Journal of Marketing Research*, 36, 2, May, 200–210.

Goldenberg, J., Lehmann, D.R. and Mazursky, D. (2001a) 'The Idea Itself and The Circumstances of Its Emergence as Predictors of New Product Success', *Management science*, Vol. 47, No. 1, January, pp. 69–84.

Goldenberg, J., Libai, B. and Muller, E. (2002) Riding the Saddle, How cross-Market Communications Creates a Major Slump in Sales, *Journal of Marketing*, Vol. 66, 2, (April), pp. 1–16.

Goldenberg, J., Libai, B. and Muller, E. (2001b) 'Talk of the Network: A Complex Systems Look at the Underlying Process of Word-of-Mouth', *Marketing Letters*, 12:3, pp. 209–21.

Granovetter, M.S. (1973) 'The Strength of Weak Ties', *American Journal of Sociology*, 78, 6 (May), 1360–1380.

Malthus, T.R. (1820) *Principles of Political Economy*, London, John Murray.

Mayer, R.E. (1999) *Fifty years of creativity research*. In: R.J. Sternberg (Ed.), *Handbook of Creativity* (pp. 449–460), Cambridge University Press.

Monod, J. (1971) *Chance and Necessity*, Vintage: NY.

Moore, G.A. (1991) *Crossing the Chasm*, New York: HarperBusiness.

Rogers, Everett M. (1962) *The Diffusion of Innovations*, 1st edition, New York: Free Press.

Rosen, E. (2000) *The Anatomy of Buzz: How to create Word-of-Mouth Marketing*, Doubleday Currency, New York, pp. 21.

Rosenau, D. Milton, ed. (1996) *The PDMA Handbook of New Product Development*, John Willy & Sons, NY.

Sperry, R. (1956) *Science and Moral Priority: Merging Mind, Brain, and Human Values*, Academic Press: NY.

Verhuulst, P.F. Notice sur la Loi que la Population Suit dans son Accroissement; Correspondence Mathematique et *Physique publie par A Quetelet* 10, 113–21 (1838); (English translation in D. Smith and N. Keyfiz *Mathematical Demography*, Springer NY 333–37) 1977.

Waldorp, M.M. (1992) *Complexity*, Touchstone Books, New York.

6
Landmarks in the Mapping of International Marketing

Stanley J. Paliwoda and John K. Ryans Jnr

The international market place is constantly changing because of diverse pressures within markets, and pressures affecting the market(s) from outside. Some are within the control of the firm, some are not. Internally, within a market, we may find important socio-economic, demographic, political, administrative or legal pressures but externally there are others as well: some economic, some technological. There exist many models, which seek to address and bring these random elements together in compiling an objective country market appraisal. These models come under different names and include – among others: PEST (Political, Economic, Social and Technological), PESTEL (Political, Sociocultural, Environmental, Economic, Technological, and Legal). A further variant is SLEPT (Social, Legal, Economic, Political and Technological). Each offers a different agenda and prioritisation. They seek to incorporate random and non-random elements to facilitate decision making. These elements can exert pressure within markets. Importantly, these pressures will not all be experienced to the same degree across all developed markets, so the effects may well be different. So too, may the terminology employed, which is also constantly changing. We used to talk of 'joint ventures', now it is only of 'alliances'. Even the term 'international marketing' is not immune from change. Looking across the bookshelves in any business bookstore, you will note that many authors who had previously produced works on 'international marketing' are now producing later updated editions but with a title of 'Global Marketing'. It is not a question of scale of operations or of sophistication. The same phenomena exist internationally and present opportunities for companies of all sizes including SME's (small and medium-sized enterprises) but the scale of operations

The map of global affluence

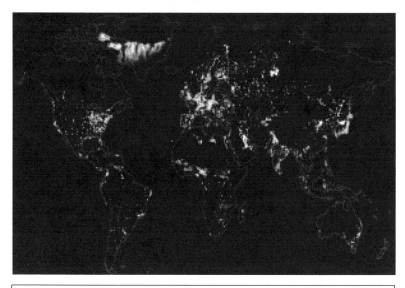

This map of the earth at night has been produced by NASA from a mosaic of about 40 separate satellite photographs. Lines have been drawn in here to identify the different continents and counties of the world. The reflected light is a result of the polar ice cap, which is clearly identifiable, there are also agricultural and forest fires and oil and gas burn-off taking place. However, the main point to be drawn from this map is that 25 per cent of the world's population consume 75 per cent of all the electricity produced. Those pockets of intense light can therefore be seen as being the places in the world where we find affluent consumer markets.

Source: Used with kind permission of NASA.
Credit: C. Mayhew and R. Simon (NASA/GSFC), NOAA/NGDC, DMSP Digital Archive.

differs markedly as it must fall in line with corporate resources. The issue though was of terminology and here is one instance where publishers are being dishonest with their public, seeking only to make their book contents more attractive and seem more advanced by adapting the book title. It is an age-old practice of following fashion but hardly ethical and not one to follow.

Now, in this essay, we choose to use the term 'international marketing' because we believe 'global marketing' to be an activity which can be practised only by the largest market players. We do not, however, wish to focus only on the most sophisticated and advanced stage of a process to the exclusion of all else. 'Global Marketing' we view as an activity, which applies only to the largest companies who have reached a stage of global stardom and now have resources as well as the need for management to be able to control their brands across many national borders. Instead of all this, we present our perspective on the international marketing environment and the tools, which can be used within this environment, irrespective of size. We believe that marketing is involved as soon as a company starts on the internationalisation process. There are few market opportunities today, which are met simply by making your product available. In most economic sectors, which have also known increasing concentration of supply in recent years, success comes only to those who have taken the time to assess their customers' needs properly and have then sought to fulfil them. Being present in an industry is on its own insufficient as a criterion for success. Presence alone or time spent in an industry or country market does not mean that any learning is taking place. It can be an entirely passive experience perhaps like the onset of age. So first, there has to be some study undertaken of the market and of the customers in it. Next, there has to be some ability to interpret the data meaningfully, and a willingness on the part of the company to implement changes that will bring the company closer to its target customers.

International marketing strategy involves balancing the costs of formulating a strategy to meet identified overseas customer needs with a realisation that despite the anticipated profitability of the venture, the risks are much higher. Consequently, the anticipated reward will have to compensate for the risks in the fundamental 'Go–No Go' decision-making situation. In this situation, knowledge of the market and of the customers in it can prove invaluable. The differences between domestic and international marketing were identified by Paliwoda (1995) in Table 6.1 reproduced in summary form below. In international marketing, the range of variables is more extensive than we would find in our own domestic market where we have knowledge not only of our own operations but of those of our competitors. Furthermore, we are also naturally attuned to existing as well as impending legislative or social changes that may require some corporate action from us. To begin with then, in the international arena, we have first to admit that our knowledge is greatly limited even of the opportunities that may be presented before us and how we might best deal with them. What passes down to us as information may be decidedly dubious, biased and occasionally seriously mistaken advice on the part of intermediaries whose interests do not naturally coincide with those of the prospective internationalist.

Viewing the totality of international operations, we now reproduce here the 10P's in Table 6.1, which include:

The variables in Table 6.1 remain outside of all these popular strategic models that we listed earlier such as PEST, SLEPT etc. There is absolutely no point in conducting an outstanding and comprehensive environmental report that omits serious study of the customers that we should be targeting now and in the future. Equally, there are many people to be found around the customer who might be influential in helping to instil some awareness or perception of our product. Favourable perceptions of the company can greatly enhance positioning of the company's products or brands. The single greatest difficulty faced by marketers is that we frequently lack hard science. Marketing data is mostly perceptual and so is judgemental. The task is then to influence perception through persuasion.

There are many things, which stand in the way of good effective communication. One is the intensity of competition across all developed market economies. We know that there are an ever-increasing number of companies all vying for our attention and our spending power. Yet another factor is that international companies if successful

Table 6.1   Domestic and international marketing – a 10 point checklist

1. People – all stakeholders internal and external to the firm, including employees and customers.
2. Process – which is unique to the corporate culture and may include willingness or not to consider a certain form of market entry such as joint venture.
3. Positioning – differentiation from rivals.
4. Power – market power transferability from home country to host country.
5. Product / Service – delivering value added through the channel to the foreign consumer.
6. Promotion and publicity – what is available, what is allowable, what is free.
7. Pricing – an overplayed dimension and the weakest factor with which to lead.
8. Place of sale / Distribution – delivery. From arrival portside to the final consumer through channels as diverse as the Internet.
9. Planning and control – with flexibility. Monitoring is one aspect but another is the ability to plan ahead with room to manoeuvre so as not to forestall strategic alternatives.
10. Precedents – learned from market scanning. Through environmental scanning at home and abroad, it is possible to discover strategies that may be borrowed from other companies in other industries or in other countries and applied to your own situation.

Source: Paliwoda, 1995

are often treated with suspicion by the media and the general public, if one does not generally follow the other. The very term 'globalisation' has become associated with rather sinister undertones. If only we were truly able to derive some coherence from the motley band of protesters who now regularly picket the World Trade Organisation (WTO) meetings, allegedly on behalf of us all and in the name of democracy. These unelected protesters then find themselves further detached from the democratic purpose, which they claim to serve than the politicians that they claim to despise. Curiously, they seem to see in the corporate world a power that is greater and more responsive than the political machine. There is always a danger of believing your own propaganda and so these anti-globalisation protesters frequently make the mistake of assuming that corporations have eternal life and do not in themselves make mistakes or act without a sinister purpose in mind. Instances such as the collapse of Enron or the Bridgestone tyres debacle that Ford experienced with their Explorer SUV (or, as may be better understood by a British audience, four-wheel drive or 4¥4), show clearly that the corporate world is equally exposed to sudden and dramatic change. No matter, as an economic activity, world trade continues to be the most effective and the single most important economic activity in terms of experiencing growth. Nevertheless, academic progress in the field of international marketing is still at least one-step behind the actual practice for a number of different reasons but largely, that of corporate confidentiality (Paliwoda 1999). Everyone wishes to secure knowledge for themselves but no one wishes to divulge any information, which may be useful to a competitor.

As a result of increasing study, we have built up a literature whereby we are now able to examine some of the landmarks in the extant literature in the light of current practice. This was something that was denied by some of those great polemical writers such as Theodore Levitt and others who were not really able to test their theories 20 and 30 years ago. Writing on globalisation in 1983, Levitt saw globalisation almost as an inevitable by-product of product standardisation. We as consumers would be willing to accept the product if it was offered to us in the name of the necessary global economies of scale rather than in terms of whether it actually offered any meaningful benefit to us as consumers.

Today, we appear to focus more on the consumer and make greater efforts to offer meaningful value to the consumer. Consumers are researched more thoroughly than before but on the other hand, we also now have the technology to enable flexible manufacturing systems to enable us to produce product variations to suit groups of customers exactly. This is in itself an important marketing milestone.

Back in 1995, we presented what we considered to be Eight Continuing and Future Challenges for companies going international. Nearly a decade later, we still see value in these predictions but also see different and more complex emergent challenges. Not that we were wrong in the first instance but over time, any situation will change and priorities and customer values have indeed changed. The original Eight included the following and they are reported here with some explanation (See Table 6.2).

Many of these challenges still remain in the market situation today. However, instead of seeking to reposition or to question an earlier summation, we decided to create a new table, viewing international marketing eight years later. We take some pride in the accuracy of our previous predictions and present here a further future framework for international marketing and a map of how we see the future unfolding for this uncertain discipline.

We predict that the future face of international marketing will be the following: We have conducted our own scan of the international marketplace and present our own listing of the present and future challenges, taking full responsibility for the accuracy, errors and omissions of the contents:

Intellectual property (IP) may become the key market entry consideration. Counterfeiting and parallel market (or grey markets) will continue to be a major irritant and market spoiler to the major global corporations. Protection of intellectual property (e.g. patents) and also industrial property rights (trademarks, brand names etc.) has been thrown into focus with the intervention of U.S. President George Bush Jr. into the availability of drugs under patent protection both in the USA and in South Africa. Big Business has to realise that if the President of the largest single market and the most powerful country in the world wants to see a change in the distribution to make pharmaceuticals more available and cheaper then it will happen, it is inevitable.

Increasing sophistication of consumers. Consumers will always be willing to pay an extra premium in return for perceived added value. This has fuelled international trade for centuries when we were dealing only with tea and spices. Today, country of origin often vies alongside branding for equal attention. Global advertising and the use of the Internet and other new media forms, yet to appear on pocket gadgets and become commonly available, will influence these new consumers of the future. At the moment, the Blackberry, which is a Bluetooth-enabled

Table 6.2 Eight continuing and future challenges

1. Economic integration. The impact of European integration within the European Union was having a formidable effect in regenerating many West European countries. It was indicated that EU membership could easily rise to 28 member states. However, while there is interest worldwide in the European experiment, other trading blocs stop at the economic stage and keep well clear of any permanent political association e.g. USA in NAFTA has loose ties with Canada and Mexico. To take the case of the EU again, it officially represents all of its member states in the negotiation of international treaties. Clearly, in terms of size and membership, APEC (Asia Pacific Economic Cooperation) spanning two continents is the largest of all and so has tremendous potential to influence world trade if ever it chooses to do so, although ironically its size appears to be preventing it from achieving consensus amongst its members. There are many other large free trade agreements worldwide, including NAFTA. Originally just Canada and the USA, Mexico was brought into the North American Free Trade Area in 1992, creating a new market of 360 million, focusing on the facilitation of trade and the elimination of tariffs and nontariff barriers including health, safety and environmental standards and regulations, intellectual property, rules of origin, and a harmonised tariff classification and dispute resolution. Beyond NAFTA, which has had some successes and some failures, talk is now focused on the FTAA (Free Trade Area of the Americas). ASEAN (Association of East Asian Nations) formed in 1967 including Indonesia, Malaysia, Philippines, Singapore, Thailand and Brunei has had some successes in diplomatic collaboration and cooperation in transport and communications but could do significantly better than it is presently doing without exceeding their original mandate which was regional collaboration. It is only the European Union that embraces political and economic union; others stop at the facilitation of trade.
2. Strategic alliances are increasing in all industries across all nations as a preferred means of corporate foreign market entry.
3. Brands are replacing products. Consumers have become increasingly sophisticated and product knowledgeable with the advent of new means of communication and the concentration of suppliers. While this has led to globalisation and product standardisation in the main, segmentation and pre-testing are still necessary. Over-standardisation in an era of anti-globalisation is a sin. All companies need a vision to follow, even start-up companies. Now, where that vision is clearly expressed in a corporate mission statement there can be no confusion amongst management, employees or shareholders alike as to what may be regarded as an appropriate action or course of corporate behaviour or even new strategic direction. Production as a central focus for management is wasteful of resources including marketing resources and can very easily and very quickly create a negative image for the company concerned. There is not a customer alive who does not wish to be treated as special and have his or her individual needs satisfied. Unlike the production function, marketing researches the market to find out the needs and wants of consumers and so we have a situation ideally where the needs of consumers are met exactly. Consumers

Table 6.2   Eight continuing and future challenges – *continued*

---

because they feel the company understands them and the brand in question meets their needs. This is quite different from indiscriminate corporate actions such as selling on price. This is a good use of resources and because it balances supply with demand, allows the company to charge a premium price.

4. Time to market is critical but product differentiation (physical and psychological) is equally important.

5. Market data are increasingly important especially for the many relatively new transitional economies. Need for awareness, image and preference data has led to new types of market research.

6. Regulation is important in a world trade order dominated not by trading nations but by economic blocs such as the European Union, which accounts for nearly 40 per cent of world trade. This has led to the establishment of a new organisation under the auspices of the United Nations, The World Trade Organisation (WTO).

7. Distribution channel change. Major changes in distribution channels e.g. concentration in retailing, use of the internet (Hamill 1997, Palumbo and Herbig 1998, Zugeleder et al. 2000) and the rise of international retailing. There is the problem of finding exclusive agents and representatives.

8. Consumer price sensitivity. Worldwide, consumers are becoming more price sensitive and so private labels are a response by retailers to ensure margins and customer loyalty.

---

mobile communications device, offers the consumer the unlimited con-nectivity that we expect of this new interactive technology. We expect not only to be updated with the news that we regard as important but also the general ability to communicate and to be heard and listened to. Yesterday's market was about one-way communication. Tomorrow's markets will involve two-way communication and greater interactivity. The opportunity is there to get involved and learn about prospective customers if companies are indeed up to the challenge and willing and able to make something of it. It is a unique opportunity and given the speed and economies of scale important in bringing products to market, connectivity alone may well decide the future as to who will be the suc-cessful market players.

Socio-demographic changes such as the 'greying of consumers'. The demographic fact is that across all developed countries the bulk of the disposable wealth is passing now into the hands of those in a large sector of the population that is either going into retirement or taking early retirement. The situation is expected to become more acute over the next 10 years when the largest single sector in society continues to wield disposable spending power from retirement. It means impending social unrest as the minority that will be in the working population have to continue to work to ensure a comfortable retirement for the retired masses. It means new goods and services will be created and that we will be required to refocus our thinking on segmenting this age group, differentiating those in retirement from those relatively young and affluent, to those who are aged and infirm. From travel and adventure to home care and residential nursing care, increasing provision will have to be made and we will have to adjust to seeing some of those Hollywood and television stars of yesteryear offering celebrity endorsements for those new products and services for the old.

Free trade will always remain a political 'hot potato' but we have to realise that no one nation will ever wish to participate in totally free trade. The next best thing if we can ever hope to reach agreement will be an international understanding on 'freer' trade. The facilitation of trade, the harmonisation of tariffs, the introduction and legal acceptance of electronic signatures are all issues of our present day. The economic effects of EU enlargement may be politically challenging but it has been said that the combined effect of a further 10 countries joining the EU in 2004 will only amount to the economic significance of a country the economic size of the Netherlands joining the Union. Compared to the current EU membership, the new entrants are not very advanced economies in their own right and present some challenges in terms of the subsidies, which they may fight to receive. However, looking beyond the European dream there is a very real prospect of a new market reality that is truly borderless and more transparent than ever before. There will be opportunities for small countries as well as for small companies to make inroads in such areas as commodities. Examples may be found in trade between Canada and the US and Chile and the US.

Euro brands will expand with the increase in cross border mergers and acquisitions in retailing. Similarly, we expect to see a greater presence of 'own label' brands in retail stores across North America, which has been much slower than Europe in opening up to this phenomenon, which reflects the power shift that has taken place from manufacturer to retailer. The concentration that has been taking place at the retail level poses a threat to manufacturers and to SME's particularly. For traditional brands, maintaining awareness can only be attained if there is cost minimisation taking place somewhere in the channel. This then ultimately drives the brand overseas to be manufactured and then reimported for sale. It begs the question as to whether there is only a loss leader future for some brands? Are companies simply being narcissistic in the pursuit of brands where ultimate price control is out of their grasp? At the same time, China, which has become a major source of manufacturing, has been supplying goods for sale under different established brand names. We can expect then to see both China and India developing their own brands within developed markets. It is a small start but Rover (UK) has already announced an alliance with Tata of India whereby they are soon to offer Indian cars for sale in the U.K.

Marketing to be outsourced. We have witnessed various facets of the advertising industry becoming specialist and then separated from the mainstream. We can expect to see marketing being outsourced in future.

Foreign market control of assets has always been something to be feared, almost as though it were a form of blackmail. There was no alternative but to pay what was being asked and perhaps then this blackmailer might go away? Well, the parallel is not even close for anyone serious about market entry as they have to consider being in that market for the long term. Going away is not an option. Instead, we should see 'psychological closeness' with suppliers increasingly becoming a consideration.

Alliances will be tested. There has been a tremendous growth in alliances over the last 10 to 15 years. In an economic downturn, we can expect alliances to be the first to go. Having said that, we do not envisage an economic downturn within the next five years. The stock markets are still readjusting and making a correction to the over-inflated prices that existed during what will henceforth be known as the 'Enron era' when stocks were grossly and fraudulently inflated and there was no substance to the figures presented to financial publics. The business schools came off lightly in that debacle which followed.

Breaking the cycle or changing reflex reactions. Mindsets are difficult to change. In downturns, we always hear of cutbacks to marketing and training, the two key areas most likely to lead to a speedy economic recovery. Will common sense ever prevail?

Cost minimisation, the strategy favoured by accountants who take charge of the marketing function will continue to vie for supremacy with the optimal service levels mooted by marketers. Cost minimisation can never hope to become an enticing and attractive strategy to customers who only see the company stripping out costs and adding nothing in return for customers. It will never win new customers whereas an attractive customer service level most definitely will do so.

Individual corporate action. Information has become a free good. It should be possible for a company to search out markets for itself and not play 'follow my leader'; simply going into markets after the competition has already entered. To do so denies the effect of the 'first mover advantage' but more importantly, it is just dumb. Companies should make their own decisions and be prepared to take courageous decisions for themselves. The BEM's (Big Emerging Markets) identified by the U.S. Department of Commerce are not the sum total of all worthwhile markets worldwide nor are they suitable for all sizes of company with differing levels of international experience.

Transitional economies and emergent economies, by whatever term we choose to call them, should be expected to account for a larger and increasing share of world trade and a higher value component in their exports. It should also be emphasised that the term 'transitional' means that we do not expect these economies to stay in this state for long but to progress quickly. The WTO Ministerial conference in Cancun in 2003 broke up in disarray but it united the developing countries in a way that had never been seen before. These countries that became known as a grouping called G21 have a future if they continue to function in a united way and so should be able to influence future WTO policy and start to see some economic gains.

Regulation. On the one hand, there will always be the need for international standardisation but national economic self-interest will continue to prevail as an important and decisive factor. The future of the WTO and the ability of the developing countries to make a concerted effective stand will determine the future regulation of world trade.

Foreign media to follow foreign products? There have always been some international publications such as the Economist, which takes international advertising, but the opportunities now abound with a whole range of media opportunities from Internet to satellite television to digital radio to print media. This has not been truly exploited. There is convergence taking place already but for this to become effective we would need to ensure that there is a global market segment and an infrastructure to allow it to happen. Even with satellite television, there is some television advertising that has to be blocked for certain countries because of national codes of advertising practice. Most advertising regulation is voluntary and self-policing but the dangers in seeking to run counter to this are very great particularly in a world economy where words spoken in Birmingham, England, can become widely known the next day in Melbourne, Australia. Companies have to be aware that global communications surround them and so companies should choose to ride with the media than seek to control them.

National competitiveness inside economic groupings such as the EU remains a thorny issue. On the one hand, there is the traditional national export credit agency but on the other, there is competition also from other export credit agencies from across the EU member states. Coface from France has won a great deal of export credit finance business that traditionally went to the ECGD in Britain. Previously these were all state monopolies, now this is an area open to competition. On the other hand, national competitiveness appears to be increasingly circumscribed because of economic or political or simply custom groupings advocating free trade.

The future of the Euro currency? It has created transparency of pricing which has been welcomed by some and attacked predictably by others, but will it be only for internal sales within the EU or will it become an international currency? 10 more countries join in 2004 but will Britain ever join the Euro Zone? The effects either way could be very dramatic.

International trade financing will continue to require innovative thinking. Countertrade and leasing were innovative when they first appeared. The continuing pressures to do business will force the creation of further enabling financial tools to be devised.

E-Commerce has very successfully created new opportunities for the individual but it has been outstandingly successful in creating the web auction. This has meant a coming together of buyers and sellers as seen in E-Bay but also the Dutch Flower Auction and Covisint, a grouping of five automobile manufacturers and their worldwide suppliers, currently numbering 76,000, which was established only in February 2000. This interactive medium allows for live transactions and so is sure to change the way in which we do business in an industry that has always been international in outlook.

International Marketing for a Service Economy:

Negative
- Lack of identity
- Call centres (overseas?)
- Manufacturing
- Outsourcing (quality?)
- Lack of tangibility
- Perishability – if no one knows about you, will they care when you are gone?

Positive
- Global franchising
- Free trade in services allows universities for example to export degree programmes

The world is not going to change greatly in the years ahead but we can expect as ever before the presence of discontinuous change, which will require managers to retain an agile mind and organisations to be flexible. As has always been the case in the past, the spoils will always go to the winners. There are no consolation prizes in business. Markets are most unforgiving yet at the same time, we have to realise the new realities of world opinion. There are tensions and there is public nervousness about big businesses but equally, we can see measures on important yardsticks such as poverty, education, general literacy and life expectancy showing improvements year on year. Globalisation in the main has been good for people. At the same time, marginalisation has been the real threat to the world's poor and this has been emphatically stated by the former Director General of the WTO, Michael Moore. The world is changing. Manufacturing has followed agriculture and has moved to the developing countries and the world's biggest industry is now tourism, which at least provides an assurance for the necessary preservation of local cultures. Elsewhere it is becoming increasingly important to seek to protect product names that have been around for quite some time as the New World seeks to export to the Old World. Names like Chardonnay and Cheddar may be seen as traditional product types but what is different today, is the provenance of these products. These products are now being supplied to the Old World by the New World, creating thereby a rush by the Old World to protect even common generic names from universal usage. Whisky and champagne were amongst the earliest examples to achieve protection but there is now a flood of similar applications pending. We may now have a WTO but in reality, we respond to perceived trade threats as ever before, by protectionism and through subsidies.

Case 1 – Mecca Cola: a political tool or a commercial product?

When asked to name a global brand, Coca Cola would undoubtedly feature strongly in any response. It has had its competitors over time but the brand has successfully sustained repeated and ongoing attack due to the popularity of its mainstay brand. There are now new competitors on the block appealing to Arab and Muslim sentiment. On the one hand, the Middle East is said to represent only 2 per cent of Coca Cola's revenues but the competitive threat becomes more real once Western markets with large Muslim communities start to open up to the incoming product and become committed.

New competitors include the Iranian drink, Zamzam Cola, named after a holy spring in Mecca, which has been successful in Saudi Arabia and Bahrain. This was developed as a replacement for American soft drinks after the 1979 Islamic revolution in Iran and is exported to Iraq, Pakistan and some African countries and looks set to expand its operations worldwide. Another competitor on the scene is British-made Qibla Cola, a name that refers to the direction Muslims face when praying to Mecca. Its slogan is 'liberate your taste'. However, what has captured most attention has been Mecca Cola and the question now being asked is whether this is going to be in any way different from other competitors who have come and gone? This new competitor was founded by a French Tunisian entrepreneur who has stated on BBC News that 'our proposal is more political than commercial'. Its founder claims the drink is not competition for Coke but is expected to sell very well during the Muslim holy month of Ramadan and that his campaign is not anti-American but anti-Bush Administration. They scored a public relations coup by dubbing themselves sponsor of the 1 million strong peace march in London on February 15, 2003 and handing out 36,000 bottles of Mecca Cola and 10,000 t-shirts with the Mecca Cola logo and the message 'Stop the War' and 'Not in my Name'. They also had a vehicle with a 20-foot high Mecca Cola can pulling a trailer with an outdoor board saying: 'All human beings are born free and equal...and should think before they drink'.

Coca Cola has high visibility as a quintessentially American product and has consequently become a lightning rod for international dissatisfaction against the USA. Timing in terms of bringing a product to market is everything and so we have to concede that the war in Iraq has polarised opinion around the world and created many disaffected groups who are now seeking alternatives to American products such as the ubiquitous Coca-Cola.

Competition in any market segment worth entering is relentless. In previous cola wars, price, product, appearance, and channels of distribution have all been tried before and have failed. Mecca Cola is a new entrant with a higher chance of success than previous competitors because of its ability to play upon anti-US sentiment and unite a large Muslim market spread over very many markets. In addition, it benefits from being seen as a 'David' to Coca Cola's 'Goliath' and at the same time being seen to support local charities as well as the Palestinian cause. In terms of promotion, it appeals directly to all outside the Northern hemisphere but also to very many inside, with a rather tongue in cheek anti-American orientation in a product that is designed to look very similar to its American market leader. The colour, the labelling, the font and the logo are designed to be similar while different, for the logo of Mecca Cola translated from the French is, 'No more drinking stupid, drink with commitment' and 'Don't shake me, shake your conscience'. It makes great play of the 10 per cent of profit that goes to Palestinian charities and 10 per cent to European NGO's. This appeals of course to its target audience but has also led to a boycott of the product in France where it originated. However, this is unlikely to really affect its sales, in fact quite the opposite, it is likely to give this product further free promotion and establish it firmly in the market as an alternative to the real thing. This product is seen as filling a gap and is well placed to take advantage of a hitherto weak Arab boycott against Coca Cola. However, we know little of how this product actually measures up in taste tests and whether once the initial political protest has been made, whether the quality is sufficient to sustain the Mecca Cola brand longer term.

Mecca Cola draws its support from many areas. Consumers want to find non-American alternative brands and Mecca Cola makes a very bold statement that has caught the imagination of Muslims everywhere. It is bold, it gives to charity and it encourages its consumers with its radical slogan and donations to charity. It appeals to those who might be attracted by the political statement but it has also become fashionable. The entrepreneur behind Mecca Cola maintains that it is not an anti-American stance but an anti-Bush administration stance. While some are very approving of this new product, some religious fundamentalists object to the presence of holy place names on branded products, irrespective of origin. Sacrilege is sacrilege, no matter where you live or what you believe.

Meanwhile, the boycott on American goods is having an effect and the switching costs for consumers when it comes to soft drinks are negligible. Muslim campaigners object to the economic ties with Israel (Coca Cola opened a plant in Israel in the 1960's) and the war on terror has made all American products a target and a focus for resentment. Disaffected people buy Mecca Cola because they feel it is the only protest that they can make. The brand could become a tool to hit America but this competitive battle cannot be fought on politics or religion. It is easy for consumers to express their politics simply by switching brands. Britain has 1.8 million Muslims; France has 5 million – the largest Muslim population in Western Europe. Presently, Mecca Cola is sold in the UK with a large distribution base in Birmingham. In France, the supermarket chain, Auchan, is now stocking the brand, and it is also on sale in Belgium and Germany. There are dangers of stigmatisation and of politicisation of trade. US firms fear a greater backlash still against US brands. This may well happen but whether it will be sustained will depend upon the product quality behind the marketing and ultimately, how consumers respond.

Source: Case Mecca Cola developed by the authors from secondary sources as indicated below.

Case Notes

Jeffrey, Simon (2003, February 5), 'Is it the real thing?', *Guardian Unlimited*, Retrieved 26 September 2003 from http://shopping.guardian.co.uk/food/story/0,1587,889470,00.html

Hutton, Will (2003, April 20), 'Goodbye Coke, Hello Mecca Cola', *Washington Post*
Retrieved 26 September 2003 from http://www.washingtonpost.com/ac2/wp-dyn/A54023-2003Apr18?language=printer
Britt, Bill (2003, February 24), 'Mecca Cola mimics Coke: Sales support Palestinians', *AdAge.com*
Retrieved 26 September 2003 from http://www.adage.com/news.cms?newsId=37207
Martin, Sarah (2002, December 5), 'France: Cola Drink hopes to cash in on anti-Americanism', *Radio Free Europe/ Radio Liberty*
Retrieved 26 September 2003 from http://www.rferl.org/nca/features/2002/12/05122002171916.asp
Henley, Jon and Jeevan Vasagar (2003, January 8), 'Think Muslim, drink Muslim says new rival to Coke', *Guardian Unlimited*
Retrieved 26 September 2003 from http://www.guardian.co.uk/international/story/0,3604,870413,00.html
Bittermann, Jim (2002, November 6), 'Boycott battle meets cola wars', *CNN.com*
Retrieved 26 September 2003 from http://edition.cnn.com/2002/WORLD/europe/11/05/mecca.cola/
BBC News World Edition (2002, May 21), 'Islamic cola benefits from boycott',
Retrieved 26 September 2003 from http://news.bbc.co.uk/2hi/middle_east/2000574.stm
BBC News World Edition (2002, August 21), 'Islamic cola selling well in Saudi',
Retrieved 26 September 2003 from http://news.bbc.co.uk/2/hi/middle_east/2207565.stm
Murphy, Verity (2003, January 8), 'Mecca Cola challenges US rival',
Retrieved 26 September 2003 from http://news.bbc.co.uk/2/hi/middle_east/2640259.stm
Hawley, Caroline (2000, May 13), 'Muslim Cleric defends Coke',
Retrieved 26 September 2003 from http://news.bbc.co.uk/2/hi/middle_east/747575.stm

Case 2: Volkswagen's Reinvention of the International Skoda Brand

When Volkswagen bought over Skoda in 1991, it acquired an outdated auto plant and a brand that could be said to be known everywhere but a brand to which no one in the UK was favourably disposed. Skoda had a history dating back to 1895, the third oldest car plant in the world. While it had some successes in its early years, it had achieved very little in recent decades. This is an unusual case where a brand was further weakened by the image surrounding its source of origin to the point where it actually created additional positive disconfirmation. The timing of the investment in 1991 may have been opportune in terms of buying a plant in Eastern Europe following the Velvet Revolution that had just taken place. A new consumer market was now just opening up within Central and Eastern Europe and this region now looked to the democratic free markets of the West now that it was free of the militaristic control of the old Soviet Union. Foreign investors could now view market expansion opportunities within Eastern Europe and if successful, then exporting to Western Europe could also become possible but there were many problems to surmount first. These cars were bought on price not by choice, the technology was fairly primitive, the build quality was poor, there was little after sales service and support, consequently, the cars were widely known to be unreliable and so many British comedians were able to make careers out of developing jokes around the Skoda brand and its product line. Along then came Volkswagen who appear to have had a clear international marketing segmentation strategy in mind. VW management clearly perceived Skoda owners and drivers to be vastly different from those owning and driving a Seat or Audi and so they developed a successful positioning strategy for Skoda as a fourth company and a stand alone brand within the VW Group. Future growth for Skoda would be focused on Central and Eastern Europe and particularly Russia, where the brand was well known and respected and so required little promotional support as it represented very good value for money.

The starting point was to retain the Skoda brand name that was estimated to be worth £200 million in terms of recognition but it was quickly found to be more of a stigma than a brand. No matter what quality now went in to its manufacture and all the various stages of the distribution channel, it would take a lot of time and investment to undo the errors of the past. The Motoring Correspondent of the Daily Mirror in February 2000 produced a review, which outlined the task that lay ahead:

> I see that the Skoda Fabia has been named 'Car of the Year' but I somehow don't think I'm ready to drive one yet. I still think it's slightly less embarrassing to be seen getting out of the back of a sheep than getting out of the back of a Skoda.

VW had to recreate an image and reputation for Skoda through quality manufacturing, clever design and attractive styling, bundling a number of benefits within an attractive price. Clever marketing would not have worked particularly in markets which had known communist propaganda. There had to be something tangible to support the marketing claims. However, buying a car is still the second largest purchase the average consumer will make after buying a house. Consumers had not just to be tempted but to be convinced that in buying a Skoda with their hard-earned money, they were not buying a joke. However, the Skoda campaign continued with attention paid to new redesigned dealerships and a focus on developing a relationship with dealers and with the buying public to make them warm towards the Skoda brand. The motoring press were courted at the international shows and exhibitions. The advertising budget for the Fabia launch was £4.5m whereas Toyota spent £9m on the Yaris launch and Renault spent £17m on the relaunched Clio. The creative work for the advertising campaign revolved around a central thought – 'The Fabia is a car so good that you won't believe it's a Skoda'. Employing subtle, rewarding humour was key. The intention was to get people to feel that they were in on the joke, subtly moving them onto Skoda's side.

Independent research also showed a watershed change of opinion. Before February 2000, sixty percent of consumers polled said that they would not consider buying a Skoda. After the launch campaign, consideration of Skoda models rose by over 50%, which equates to over 1 million more potential Skoda drivers. Skoda's image rocketed. The same research showed that before February 2000, a modest 54% of respondents agreed that Skodas are better than they used to be. After February 2000, this figure climbed to 79%.

The Skoda Fabia became 'European Car of the Year' twice. The Superb became 'Tow Car of the Year 2003' and Scottish Writers' 'Luxury Car of the 2003'. Skoda has produced 4 million cars since it was taken over by the VW Group in 1991. The friendly image of the brand continues to be projected in the website: www.skoda-auto.com , which contains a section labelled 'fun' as well as a children's section and many screensaver and wallpaper downloads as well. Skoda has now firmly established itself as a manufacturer of quality albeit with a rather quirky, idiosyncratic image but one, which is customer friendly. There has been a significant change in the public's perception of Skoda and the brand image has improved. The answer lies in Volkswagens' investment which allowed it to produce high quality, technologically advanced cars, the integrated communications strategy with public relations and marketing working well together to tell the same story with consistent messages and the retailer network which created the highest ever repeat purchase level for Skodas. The story of continuing improvement and investment carries on with the planned launch of further models into the future.

Source: Used with the kind permission of Cathy Bell, Head of Press and Public Relations for Skoda Auto UK.

References

Hamill, J. (1997) 'The Internet and International Marketing', *International Marketing Review*, 14 (5) pp. 300–323.

Paliwoda, S.J. (1995) *The Essence of International Marketing*, Prentice Hall, Hemel Hempstead (also available in Spanish).

Paliwoda, S.J. (1999) 'International Marketing: An Assessment', *International Marketing Review*, Vol. 16, No. 1.

Palumbo, F. and Herbig, P. (1998) 'International Marketing Tool: The Internet', *Industrial Management and Data Systems*, 98 (6), pp. 253–261.

Zugeleder, M.T., Flaherty, T.B. and Johnson, J.P. (2000) 'Legal Issues associated with International Internet Marketing', *International Marketing Review*, 17(3), pp. 253–271.

7
Integrated Marketing: A New Vision

Angus Jenkinson and Branko Sain

Introduction

Asked by many whether Integrated Marketing is not simply good marketing, we argue that in today's new, evolving and competitive marketplace, it is time to see good marketing as Integrated Marketing.

Integrated Marketing cannot be completely new or original. Nearly every senior executive we have spoken to gave a similar description of it. The concept quickly makes sense, and this can only be because leading practitioners and thinkers are already engaged with these ideas. However, Integrated Marketing pulls together many existing elements of best and emerging best practice for the first time. No formal discipline of 'Integrated Marketing' has until recently existed in the academic or practitioner worlds and most of the relevant teaching, including in IMC and CRM, is inevitably based on case evidence and empirical research with small samples, albeit with a desire to reach beyond the traditional view of the marketing disciplines. Undoubtedly, marketing has evolved into a series of relatively independent tools with different planning and evaluation criteria. Integrated Marketing not only overcomes the fragmentation of the recognised marketing disciplines but it also draws on other disciplines such as lean management, knowledge management and organisation development. It is, arguably, a natural progression of the effects of relationship marketing (Christopher et al. 1991) and CRM (Jenkinson 1995) on organisation change (Whiteley 1991), as well as developing concepts of marketing planning, e.g. Lauterborn (1990) who suggests moving from the 4Ps to 4Cs, representing increased customer focus.

The research evidence includes not only established end emerging theoretical and evidence based best practice from the UK and around the world, but also our research into over 25 major brands, including IBM, Olympus, Royal Bank of Scotland, Centrica, and the Automobile Association, the National Trust, Novartis, Amazon, and AOL, exciting niche organisations and leading agency networks. It is also based on best practice projects with significant groups of senior marketers (sponsored by the Chartered Institute of Marketing) and a diagnostic tool developed by the Centre for Integrated Marketing that indicates over 100 key pressure points. The evidence is that Integrated Marketing overturns several well-established assumptions, and constitutes a fresh vision and an enhanced challenge for both marketing leaders and other senior executives, including the CEO.

Integrated Marketing is a holistic discipline developing congruent, sustainable and high-value brand experience for all stakeholders.

This is fundamentally positive and healthy: it is positive in attitude, and it is positive in its results. In this respect, it accords perfectly with the culture of marketing at its best.

It corresponds closely with the fourth stage of IMC as formulated by Kitchen and Schultz (2000). However, it explicitly develops their suggestion of the importance and practice of cultural and organisational alignment as well promoting a mental and systemic infrastructure for integration. With the practice guidelines that it formulates, marketers undoubtedly have the potential to step up to a challenge that amounts to a widening of their responsibility, potential and vision.

A vision of Integrated Marketing

A blockbuster 90-second TV ad by Saatchi & Saatchi dating from the merger of two leading UK banks, Lloyds and TSB was launched in 1999 to 19 million people on its first showing, a mass UK audience more

Figure 7.1   What can I do (to help you)? Two life stages
Source: Used with kind permission of Lloyds and TSB.

common in previous decades. It celebrates 10 life stages from baby-hood to childbearing to uninhibited oldsters bathing naked on a beach, animated by the music of the Corrs' hit, *What can I do (to help you)?* introducing four important points about Integrated Marketing. (See Figure 7.1)

The first of these is that *the advertisement is designed to change the way people think and feel about the brand*, and a considerable investment has been put into this because it is something that really matters to both the brand, or in this case brands, and the people involved, who include not only customers but also employees and other stakeholders.

Clearly the merger of two major banks, each of which has its own her-itage and customer base, is a major marketing event and potentially one of some importance for good or ill to many millions of people. The adver-tisement's thinking, design and media schedule reflects that. It aims to plant an idea that will influence attitudes and behaviours, not only of customers but also of employees and City analysts. This idea and the emotional resonance that belongs to it are sufficiently important to justify the investment of millions of pounds. Truth to say, the idea and its resonance is worth billions; the investment question is how far such advertising would and could be effective in implanting this idea, and its resonance and credibility, in customers and other stakeholders.

The reason it has such financial power depends on the fact that the two existing banks and their future merger matters at least to some extent to their stakeholders, and in particular customers and employ-ees. How they subsequently think and feel will translate into commit-ment, behaviours and equity. We want to emphasise that we particularly include the employee here alongside the customer as an audience for this communication (Normann 1984, Reichheld 1996).

Secondly, the ad conveys a critical idea of Integrated Marketing. *Integrated Marketing is a creative, human and business discipline that is concerned with the brand being appropriately present (providing value) and effectively communicating at all the important times in a customer's life,* and in particular in the key 'moments of truth' (reflected in the 10 life-stages shown in the ad). This obviously applies as much in a business-to-business context as it does for business to consumer.

The third point follows from this. *By itself, such advertising would not work, or at best work very poorly.* In order for it and others like it to work they must be backed up in two other important ways. First, it needs to be supported by a range of other communications, including those that rein-force the message and others that provide customers with more detailed information and knowledge. Even the launch of a new soap powder needs at least the support of on-pack messaging. Similarly, employees obviously need more communication than just a commercial about what the merged organisation might mean to them, particularly since they face this future with considerably more fear than their customers. Print, for example, has permanence and detail that also reassures. This implies a harmonised, wide-media communication strategy.

Second, and more importantly, the advertising needs to be backed up by the substance and truth of the brand and its products and supporting organisation. In decades past, advertising was created live on radio. The most important advertising continues to be live, namely when customers meet the brand's people, products and services. The brand makes a promise and it has to fulfil that promise. It is therefore vital to make a promise that matters to customers but also one to which the organisation is committed. This commitment needs to include all the people that count, and that is surely everyone. Every part of the organisation communicates, even if they don't think so; therefore it becomes part of the marketing function to understand, educate and initiate positive change.

However, such commitment belongs also to the way the organisation itself is structured and focused as well as organisationally and culturally aligned by senior managers. The UK banking world has already experienced a notorious 'Listening Bank' advertising campaign from a bank that didn't, and recognises the dangers of making promises that are not based on fundamental truths of the brand. Since making attractive promises is vital to marketing, ensuring that they are or become truths is now an essential part of marketing. This represents an extension of responsibility for the discipline and individuals. For example, most of the job of the marketing director of NatWest Retail, a leading UK bank, involves this.

The final major point is that *it mattered also to the marketing teams at both Saatchi & Saatchi and Lloyds TSB* and depended on their co-operation. It represented considerable levels of time, intelligence and emotional energy invested by teams of individuals. Its launch was a moment of truth for talent, teamwork and commitment in the eyes of management, colleagues and the marketing community. The response mattered for individual careers and for the ongoing success of Saatchi and Lloyds TSB. The quality of the relationship between client and agency is an important factor in this. And this is replicated not only with every other agency-client partnership involved, from design to PR, but also in the co-ordination and relationships between them and their work.

In short, this ad introduces and implies important Integrated Marketing principles. It is about things that matter. It is a holistic discipline. At its heart is a holistic idea of communication that involves the whole business and its partners, with programmes and actions designed to change ideas, feelings and practice internally as amongst customers. Finally, Integrated Marketing serves the whole business and all its stakeholders. It is a relational discipline concentrated on creating value.

Healing the current fragmented marketing world

The need for Integrated Marketing derives from the enormously fragmented world of the modern large organisation and its stakeholder experience, well documented by organisation development (Lievegoed B. 1991), human resources and service marketing literature and research into both employee and customer satisfaction and this is supported by the research of the Centre for Integrated Marketing:

- A customer rings one support centre, identifies himself, including finding a serial number for a computer only to be told that he needs to phone a different number to get the service he wants. The entire call centre sign in process then has to be followed a second time as well as a full process of identifying himself as if this was a customer who had never contacted the brand before.
- A customer phones up a bank to speak to her relationship manager and is asked if she banks at that branch.

These are examples, among many, of fragmented customer experience. Others could include the difference between the advertisement and the actual product or service, the service during the sales process and after purchase, or the need for a professional to talk to several different sales people from the same company in order to get the consultancy support he or she needs. This is, for example, a commonplace in the Pharmaceuticals and Health industry.

But, these are not the only examples. If you are an employee in one of these large modern organisations, you have probably been through downsizing and re-engineering, been merged and reorganised a few times, assuming you've stayed long enough. From this you are expected to deduce that the brand cares about its customers and employees and has a vision of lifetime value and long-term care. Each major initiative is likely to last less than six months but you are expected to be convinced that the organisation has a long-term vision.

Your objectives tell you, if you are on the front line, for example in one of those call centres, that your job is to make the customer happy and deal with his or her problems but that you are being monitored for how long each call takes and the number of calls you handle per day. Furthermore, the hard measures of performance, including volume of calls, will be very closely tracked and applied while the soft measures may not even be measured. You might of course conclude that these competing priorities mean that the brand organisation has enormous faith in your abilities and respects your professional creativity, but it is unlikely.

In the marketing department, professionals are likely to work in product and/or marketing communication discipline silos: people who send out direct mail who have their own agency, others who create web sites, who have their own agency or agencies, others that do PR, and probably report to a different senior manager, and so on. In a large organisation this will be replicated for different product divisions. The groups may not talk to each other, or only in the most limited way, because time is short and objectives do not require it. It is very possible that the budget would have been established, or at least partly established, for each discipline at the outset of the year and each group will be working out how it is going to deploy its ring-fenced resources to achieve a set of discreet objectives that are unlikely to be formulated in the same terms as those of the other groups.

The agencies will either operate within single disciplines, in competition with each other, or there will be an integrated agency with a series of profit centres each of which is in fact competing for a share of the client's budget. Sometimes this works in the form of a group of agencies all belonging to the same company but of course having separate management, P&Ls and objectives. Furthermore the people in these agencies as well as those in the marketing department will probably be connected to a series of different professional bodies each of which is promoting their particular discipline and to the extent that they have had any formal training it would have been restricted to marketing and marketing communications topics, and is unlikely to include broader organisation change and project management issues.

Furthermore the professional marketer's training will have been fragmented into fields such as: CRM or direct marketing, service marketing, retail marketing, business to business or consumer marketing, industrial marketing, advertising, PR and so on. It is not impossible that they have been told that PR is not part of marketing. If they have had any training in Integrated Communications (IMC) either at

University or on a subsequent course, it is probable that this included a relatively brief initial overview and relatively simplistic planning framework followed by a series of isolated discourses on the practices and potential of each of the disciplines/media. They would have been told that you cannot (by definition) advertise by mail (because mail is not an advertising discipline) and that there is something enormously different between a direct response ad in a magazine, a general advertisement in the same magazine and a product placement PR feature that includes a contact telephone number to buy the product. The complexities within current marketing theory are illustrated by Jenkinson and Sain (2002a), and by Kitchen 2003a , 2003b).

To top it all, your brand may have a new marketing director every 14 months and a chief executive almost as often. However these are long tenure people compared with shareholders who are likely to hang around between 40 and 60 days. Your new top executive will be seeking to prove himself or herself rapidly and this will of course mean demolishing lots of old values and projects and creating new ones on the basis of rapid analysis and prior attitudes.

All of this might seem like a nightmare, yet while there are numerous exceptions these scenarios are undoubtedly all too common. They point to an endemic fragmentation problem. Marketers are fond of discussing media fragmentation. Compared with organisational fragmentation and the fragmentation of 'mental technology', i.e. the conceptual tools, this is probably a small problem.

Does Integrated Marketing Work?

Clearly there are legacy problems. Is this just how things have to be, or is something else possible? Does Integrated Marketing really work? Can it be done? The answer is simple: it is hard, like most worthwhile things, but it can be achieved and the results are dramatic as demonstrated by SEEBOARD Energy, a utility formed with only two million customers, which after the deregulation of the UK power industry found itself in a bitter and competitive battle for customers (Jenkinson and Sain 2003b).

Outspent by its competitors, SEEBOARD had a small share of voice. None of its customers had ever consciously chosen to be a SEEBOARD customer. They were customers only because they happened to live in the SEEBOARD area. Now all the competitors claimed to be offering a cheaper solution, and indeed turning up at the doorstep to push their offers. During 2001, despite tremendous efforts, this led to a haemorrhage of 10,000 customers a week.

SEEBOARD turned to integrated agency archibald ingall stretton (AIS) for a solution. The brief was simple:

An honest, 12-month retention plan to cover all aspects of the SEE-BOARD Energy business. Not limited by what is currently possible. Not limited by budget.

This remarkable brief led to a remarkable Integrated Marketing plan, involving a complete company-wide transformation a year ahead of Datamonitor's international analysis (2002), which argued that most utilities fail to 'live the brand' across their organisations. Datamonitor recommended brands/organisations to 'create one engaging identity that aligns all aspects of their business', a recommendation that supports Integrated Marketing.

SEEBOARD Energy undertook such an organisation wide, comprehensive project. Substantial progress led to a virtuous circle of improvement as organisational confidence and enthusiasm and positive customer attitudes steadily reinforced each other. A powerful, integrated communication programme, within a larger Integrated Marketing project, aligned current reality, vision and the brand around SEEBOARD Energy's relentless pursuit of innovative ideas that would save customers energy. The essence of the solution was based on a fundamental truth of the brand. That is why it worked. Yet, by making a promise, they created an aspirational stretch, one that lay within the organisation's potential, but only if they stepped up to the mark and ensured that the vision was authentically realised across the organisation. Borrowing from human psychology's self-actualisation, we could call this brand-actualisation.

Integrated Marketing works, if this project is any judge. The commitment was there, and the success has been startling, impacting everything from sales, to customer retention to customer attitudes and complaints, and even employee attitudes and behaviour, winning a significant number of awards, not only within the realm of internal and external communications, but also in training, utility business and culture development as demonstrated by these statistics from late 2002:

• According to J.D. Power and Associates, one of the leading customer satisfaction analysts, SEEBOARD Energy had the highest increase in overall satisfaction and was the only supplier to have seen a rise in their electricity supplier image score. Within gas supply, it had the highest increase on every individual satisfaction factor. This was confirmed when it came first in no less than eight of the nine categories measured in the December 2002 *Energywatch* statutory industry survey.

- Awareness of SEEBOARD Energy increased substantially and outstripped the dominant market leader British Gas by an unprecedented three to one.
- Internal attitudes changed. Ninety nine per cent of employees said they supported the new customer vision and strategy.
- These qualitative achievements translate into quantifiable business results. Customer losses were down 31–35 per cent year-on-year in each customer community. Cross-sell was up by 20 per cent. Against an industry average of 50 per cent cancellation rate for new accounts, the SEEBOARD Energy rate reduced from 40 per cent at the start of the campaign to just 27 per cent.
- They obtained extremely high direct response rates and a significant 20 per cent of the total customer base made its first conscious decision to be a SEEBOARD customer by signing up to one to of the new products.

In addition to these and a range of advertising, direct marketing, PR, industry services, National Training and other awards, three achievements sum up the effectiveness of their actions and communication programme:

1. Due to more customers and a justified premium over historic per-customer values the project was worth approximately £51 million net to the SEEBOARD Energy business when it was acquired by the LE Group at the end of 2002.
2. The internal transformation reduced staff churn to an all-time low so that the business saved approximately £800,000 in reduced recruitment and training costs during 2002, savings converted into marketing budget.
3. Innovation has led to new products and services that give it enduring competitive strength.

Principles of Integrated Marketing

The SEEBOARD Energy project demonstrates several important principles of Integrated Marketing:

1. The agency was a vital catalyst and extremely influential factor in the successful development of the company. For example, the

transformation was driven by its research into customer and employee attitudes and experience, brand values and also organisational competence and culture. This research was then transformed into positive insights that could drive both integrated marketing communications and organisation development. However, their insight and integrated communication worked because of the total organisation-wide commitment deriving from the leadership team and involving everyone in the company.

2. Unlike many organisations, SEEBOARD Energy internal structure is wholly aligned to delivering value to customers. In SEEBOARD Energy's case, the organisation is channelled through two customer facing groups, with each tailored to a customer community, namely residential and business customers. The whole business is designed to fit into customer sales and service. The transformation project strengthened this focus.

3. The whole organisation, and in particular all managers worked intensively on the process of change and on crafting their vision, every word of which mattered and had meaning. This customer vision is now also the basis of the brand promise: 'Passionate about finding new ways to save you energy and give even better value for money'.

4. Human resources is seen as an organisation development (OD), not personnel management, function. The OD leadership team implemented a substantial internal programme of organisation development and alignment, Programme I (for innovation). This involved everyone in the company and included new product development; internal two-way communication events; training; and auditions to take part in the new advertisements (over 100 staff members took part in the advertisements). (Technology served the organisation but was not the crucial factor here.)

5. The marketing communications project was based on a creative play between the customer vision of value and a media neutral creative idea. It included a comprehensive internal and external communication plan across all media and customer Touchpoints, from redesigning the logo to new products, television to direct mail, call centres to service engineers, with diverse creative treatments that still reflected the integrity of their creative idea. Marketing communication and OD budgets were shared and all activities were designed in collaboration. For example hundreds of employees auditioned and took part in the advertisements.

6. Finally, the relationship between agency and client was from the outset based on trust and partnership, as was the teamwork between

senior leaders across the organisation, and it shows that many ways. Partnership has been the hallmark of all successful cases that we have seen, and frankly it is hard to envisage great Integrated Marketing where this is not the case. We have certainly seen the reverse: where conflict leads to dysfunctional performance and costs.

SEEBOARD demonstrates that Integrated Marketing works and agencies can play a real part.

Why wholeness makes Integrated Marketing creative

The SEEBOARD Energy example demonstrates how Integrated Marketing is a holistic concept of communication that involves the whole business. In contrast to the fragmentation problems outlined above, integration implies wholeness. A hologram helps to illumine 'wholeness'. If you cut or tear a photograph or painting the image becomes divided or fragmented. This is because the image is not present in every part of itself. However, if you cut a hologram, the whole picture is still present. It does not matter how small the piece is, the whole picture or image remains, although the resolution is reduced. This is because the whole image is contained in every part of it, just as the whole brand is present to the customer in every Touchpoint.

Marketers routinely recognise this, that customers form an appreciation of the meaning of the brand (to them) in each Touchpoint or Moment of Truth. This means that the whole organisation and brand is present at each of its manifestations and this is not simply figurative or metaphorical. Just as the meaning progressively develops in a text, so does the meaning of the brand with successive experience either by an individual or across individuals. We can say that with more experience the resolution increases, but from the first experience the consumer forms a whole impression. We might wish to deny the truth of their experience, but the truth is that their experience is the truth for them.

Wholeness is clearly related to identity and is a fundamental part of nature. Every cell of the organism contains the image of the whole organism in the form of DNA coding. This is a fertile idea for creativity. It is characteristic that diverse works of art by a single author, poet, painter, or composer typically demonstrate his or her distinctive style and identity. Their work may be varied, but we regard it as more remarkable when it does not appear to come from the same individual as when it does.

If we asked any artist just to copy what they had already done in order to be consistent and harmonious and recognisable and coherent (and other such terms that we might want to apply to the brand experience), we would get short shrift. Integration does not require copying and repetition. It does not mean taking an image from TV and putting it in the press or mail. It does not mean that we can't, but this is not the goal. But it does mean having a strong identity.

Nature shows the creativity and metamorphosis of true identity. These leaf silhouettes all belong to a single delphinium (see Figure 7.2).

It is clear that these individual and distinct forms all *belong together*: a single creative identity has formed them. This is characteristic of nature: unity in multiplicity or diversity shows up in the millions of distinctly different trees that can all be recognised as oaks, in the diversity of snowflakes that are still snowflakes and human faces that are still human faces.

It is such creativity expressing a unifying principle that we think is the essence of Integrated Marketing. We have seen all too many examples of IMC where integration automatically means taking the same image and sticking it in different media and indeed different countries and cultures willy-nilly. This is indeed opportunistic, but sterile, insofar as customers are concerned, even when there are good creative or very strong budgetary reasons for it. Integrated Marketing should be fertile. Instead of 'repetition' let us think of harmony and variations on a theme. Perhaps even instead of 'consistency', let us think of coherence or integrity.

Figure 7.2   Leaves from a single delphinium
Source: Henri Bortoft, *The Wholeness of Nature* (1996). Reproduced with the author's permission.

This is also why brands need an empowering organising idea. Front-line staff need creative freedom and enterprise in order to respond to real needs rather than going bureaucratically by the book. When they have internalised the values and purpose of the brand, they can respond according to the principle of creative alignment (Jenkinson and Sain 2003c).

There are therefore five reasons why we believe that wholeness is a fundamental organising idea for Integrated Marketing.

1. Firstly because there is ample evidence that customers take their individual experiences as elements of the whole and use this to read the nature of the whole brand or organisation. Effectively, every interaction or Touchpoint is a unit of meaning, a hieroglyph of the organisation. Therefore, every part of the organisation, from packaging to people, matters and needs to be creatively aligned. Furthermore, there is evidence that the parts that ultimately matter most, especially for customers, are the live, reality media.

2. Secondly, communication to customers does not have the divisions for them that they have for us, the professionals. They do not evaluate communication by our different criteria, such as ads by emotional attitude and direct mail by response. It is true that they may have an emotional response to one and make a sales response to the other, but this does not mean that they compartmentalise their experience. Their response is also holistic: thinking, feeling and intention plays in each time, even if it only amounts to a dismissal. Furthermore, every single decision is ultimately based on an emotional judgment; surprising, as it may be, that is how judgments are actually made. However rational the argument, it is all designed to lead to the point where the buyer wants to buy or becomes comfortable to buy, which is an emotional response.

3. The organisations that are most successful are those that achieve fertile coherence across the organisation and its communication. This results in alignment, integration and identity and is a product of creativity not copying. A powerful way to achieve this is through vital organising ideas becoming embedded and ingrained in every part and person. However these need to be integral to the character of the organisation.

4. Organisations don't have rigid boundaries, nor does the integration challenge. 'The whole organisation' is an exploratory concept that senior executives would do well to review and discuss. Organisational and brand coherence should as far as possible extend

back through the supply chain and forward through the delivery channels as well as across the organisation. It should also extend to the customer community. Customers are participants in the wider brand organisation and its identity, and sometimes major participants:

- IBM solutions are implemented in collaboration with the client's own expertise and resources. Investment in knowledge and expertise in IBM technology by its customers contributes to IBM brand equity and customer loyalty.
- Harley-Davidson's customer tribes are part of the brand's missionary forces. Visit Olympus chat rooms on the Web, or start discussing with a photographer and it is easy to see the advertising value of their brand-loyal customers.
- British Gas customers leave their keys with the organisation to facilitate service. Such trust includes British Gas in the customer's inner circle and contributes to corporate efficiency.
- National Trust members are just that: members, and today they are the largest membership body in the UK. Thousands of them are also volunteers. The UK's Automobile Association is also a membership body, and it is this distinctive difference that makes its brand extensions such as insurance so successful.
- Weleda provides healthcare and body therapy products. Its customers are believers and advocates. Thousands turn out at its biannual picnic and fair; their children and other constituencies contribute to its annual charity calendar and of course they recommend the products, not only to other customers but even to potential stockists.

Customers contribute to market research, wear the T-shirt, display the wrapper or bag, use the product, and promote the brand values. At J. Sainsbury, a leading supermarket chain, customer investment in 'Sainsbury know-how' is vital to both their shopping experience and its brand equity and profitability.

5. There is a natural tendency for customers to coalesce around the identity of an individual brand in the category based on their general tastes and needs. It is only when the brand loses its way and identity that this degrades. This is one reason why 'community' rather than 'segments' should be the primary organising idea of marketing (Jenkinson 1994, 1995). Segmentation is necessary, but it defines divisions. We need to know what really unites consumers in

their relationship with the brand in order to produce better-tailored value propositions and to more effectively respect individual needs and situations in one-to-one communication. Community, in all its forms (flocks of birds, schools of fish, customers) is a concept of wholeness.

6. Finally, Integrated Marketing means moving from a transactional view of the customer relationship to a whole relationship view. Brands that optimise acquisition, sales and retention as a whole with their profitable customers can significantly increase profitability (Reichheld 1996, Jenkinson 1995). Too many focus excessively on acquisition, lose track of individual customers or treat the relationship as a series of individualised transactions, rather than recognising and responding appropriately to individual customers and their business history wherever they interact with the organisation. Designing and executing creative, joined-up communication programmes to replace transactional communication is another key feature of relationship management. All this requires competency in technology and data, as well as creative thinking and a culture of care. Amazon is a superb example of a company that intelligently recognises each customer, seeking to maximise the creative opportunity of each Touchpoint, as well as using permission based marketing to proactively enhance the relationship (Jenkinson and Sain 2003d). Sainsbury have developed a programme of communication with mothers, which is designed to add mutual value to the relationship (Jenkinson and Sain 2003e).

Ideas are design tools for integration

Ideas are design tools, vital for integration yet often the cause of fragmentation. They are equally significant internally, in organisation alignment, and externally, in integrated marketing communications. Furthermore, it matters whether the sets of ideas, used internally and externally are consistent and mutually reinforcing. For ideas are the driving force of the brand and business. They are embedded everywhere, showing up in policies, values and culture, in the design principle behind processes, structure and product design, in business decisions and choices, in strategies, and your brand communications, and in the meaning behind what is actually done. You can and should audit these, and you can, with difficulty, change them. The means to do this is with better ideas, and the organisations and people who have them will be the leaders of the future.

Ideas are the means by which we know things. All ideas are therefore organising ideas. The fundamental nature of an idea is to organise the mind. Similarly, the way to organise a company or its communications is also through ideas.

Ideas are not simply the product of what we see: they are part of the process of seeing. The act of seeing is also an act of meaning making, and the meaning making doesn't follow after the seeing but is part of the very seeing process itself. We do not see a tree and then conclude that it's a tree, we can see 'a tree' because it means *tree* to us. It is only afterwards that we conceptualise and rationalise about this and say 'I see'. The idea organises the seeing. Thus, human beings know the world through ideas and these ideas organise how they know the world. The organising idea of a company, if it is powerful enough, changes the world.

The most important of all organising ideas for marketers, at least at the moment, is 'the brand'. 'Brand' serves the marketing community as a focus for creative development, strategy, business organisation and so on. The reason why it is so effective in doing this is because the brand also serves as an organising idea for consumers (and also customers, channel partners and so on). One of the key purposes of advertising is to communicate an organising idea that will influence how the customer perceives the brand.

> When someone sees a Nike or IBM product, the brand serves as an organising idea that fashions his or her attitudes. Even more potently, we can say that people see Nike products in a Nike way and they see IBM products in an IBM way.

Ideas can organise, and by implication, they can disorganise. The word 'company' derives from the Italian, meaning *with bread*, or those who break bread together. A company divided ceases to be a true company. Take the example of the UK's leading auto services firm, the Automobile Association (Jenkinson and Sain 2003f), which has for a number of years used the strapline: *the fourth emergency service*, an idea that works perfectly for its large emergency-service division but less well for insurance, publishing, vehicle assessment and dozens of other services. Research showed that this powerful organising idea was actually counter-productive because it privileged one part of the organisation at the expense of others. The millions spent on it were actually leading to confusion externally and resentment internally.

Research by M&C Saatchi found that the unifying theme was: The AA rescues you from uncertainty. Adopting this idea led to re-branding of the AA with a new strapline: Just AAsk, facilitating coherence and congruence through an extensive makeover and change project, involving everything from vans to letterheads to internal marketing and training as well as external marketing communications.

This is a strong clue as to why marketers/marketing should be actively involved in the process of corporate development and organisation alignment that enables Integrated Marketing. Imaginative ideas are what people and practices, both customers and employees, can cohere. This is a true profession.

Ideas align creatively

For an organisation to achieve alignment and integration, especially a large organisation, there needs to be a powerful means to ensure that people across the organisation behave in ways that are desirable. This is essential to Integrated Marketing (Jenkinson and Sain 2002). Whereas command and control management and silos are typical as the means to achieve this alignment, in Western cultures authority alone will not and does not achieve integration. Indeed, power-based command and control management practices tend towards unhealthy, perhaps even toxic, cultures with characteristic silos, employee disaffection and high inefficiency on-costs. Widespread research clearly demonstrates this, except perhaps in cases of critical crisis (Teerlink and Ozley 2000). Even in crisis, the reason that command and control works is because it offers employees belief in a route to survive. Belief is what really matters (Jenkinson and Sain 2003g).

For sustained success, what matters is the creative fertility of individual members of the company and its functions. However this fertility must be tied together, so that, to use an old metaphor, everyone rows in the same direction. This adds up to a central principle of Integrated Marketing, which is *creative alignment*. For example, successful mission or purpose ideals have the effect of simultaneously giving clear direction and creative permission to achieve objectives.

Ghoshal and Bartlett (1998) argue that in an environment that people no longer know – or even care – what or *why* their companies are, leaders can no longer afford to focus only on refining the analytic logic that frames strategic processes. They believe that strategies can engender strong, enduring emotional attachments only when they are embedded in a broader organisational purpose. The corporate leader's greatest challenge, they argue, is to create a sense of meaning within the company, with which its members can identify, in which they share a feeling of pride, and to which they are willing to commit themselves. In short top management must convert the contractual employee of an economic entity into a committed member of a purposeful organisation.

Jesper Kunde (2002) echoes this in a marketing context:

> Some companies tend to equate branding with the company's marketing. Design a new marketing campaign and, voilà, you're on course! They are wrong. The task is bigger, much bigger. It is about fulfilling your potential ... What is my mission in life? What do I want to convey to people? How do way make sure that what I have to offer the world is actually unique? The brand has to give of itself, the company has to give of itself, and the management has to give of itself?

When this is achieved, the organisational culture trends becomes healthy: there is a sense of coherence and meaningfulness that binds people together in common purpose and in creative, learning engagement across the organisation. At the extreme, it amounts to the difference between the alignment and productivity of the chain gang versus the alignment and productivity of an Olympic rowing team.

- For Weleda UK or Lush, a producer and retailer of bathroom luxuries, who are relatively small companies in competitive environment of giants, this energy is the means to survival.
- At Olympus or IBM it means market leadership.
- At the National Trust of the National Society for the Prevention of Cruelty to Children (NSPCC) it means making a real difference.

The wholeness of Integrated Marketing therefore depends first on ideas, and in particular the organising ideas that form the identity, purpose, relationships and alignment of the organisation. Managing and cultivating these is the fundamental leadership challenge of Integrated Marketing. And the people who are most supremely gifted in technique and ability in this area must surely include senior and creative marketers.

Powerful ideas empower staff in all parts of the business. Ideas change the way people see the world. They have the potential to generate meaning and purpose. This is best achieved when there is something truly meaningful and inspiring to those concerned, which we describe as a service ideal that motivates the company.

For such an organising idea to be truly effective in achieving integration, it needs to meet five criteria. It should:

1. Be equally appropriate inside and outside the organisation, so that there is an alignment and matching of brand image and culture, internal and external messages, brand promise and organisational strategy;
2. Be meaningful and empowering, with a clearly defined purpose for which members of the company are quickly and confidently motivated to take ownership (because it matters to them) and which they can use as a benchmark for decision-making. (Note that this is not trying to motivate sluggish employees; it is channelling inherent motivation);
3. Provide considerable creative space: the definition of purpose needs to provide channels for creative energy, not boxes that squash people and motivation;
4. Include both a longer-term visionary aspect and the means to translate this into step-by-step vision;
5. Be based on the fundamental principle of quality in an integrated marketing organisation: it is only quality when it is good for the customer, good for the people doing the work, and good for the brand/company.

i2 Technologies' organising idea is value-generating

i2 Technologies' organising idea is a superb example that inspires staff, customers and analysts (Jenkinson and Sain 2002c). i2 Technologies, Inc. was founded in 1988 by Sanjiv Sidhu and Ken Sharma with the vision of helping businesses make more intelligent supply chain decisions by using information resources. Since then, i2 has become a market leader with a multinational team of nearly 5,000 employees.

The i2 leadership team created an exceptional and extraordinary, yet simple, way of focusing the company through a powerful motivating service idea:

We will create $75 billion value for our clients by 2005.

Notice, this is a very different idea from wanting to create 75 billion dollars worth of value for shareholders. Instead of serving a group of invisible market forces, whose average tenure of shares from purchase to sale in the USA is currently 44 days, it is an idea that has real meaning for the individual, the organisation and of course its customers. And of course, even the financial analysts love it, because it is undoubtedly focused on what creates sustainable shareholder value.

Everything at i2 is aligned to this idea: strategy, objectives, vision.

- The value created for i2's clients is audited and tracked by an independent agency.
- It is what the company says to analysts, prospects and customers.
- It is the focus of internal product development and training.

i2's missionary idea has inspired many of the smartest and most committed people in the industry to join the company. They did so because they could immediately see both the marketing power of the idea and its motivational value and relevance to them. A senior product manager, told us: 'To me, this was such a powerful mission that I was willing to bet my future on the company. That's why I joined.'

Thus it makes a major contribution to fashioning an organisation whose internal culture and external brand image and messaging are congruous.

Great communication needs great, media neutral creative ideas

Ideas are not only design tools for the organisation but for its external and internal communication. Integrated communication aims to achieve synergy and harmony across a variety of different media and treatment. There is evidence that this leads to not only more efficient marketing (more reach and contact per unit of cost), but also more effective marketing, for example through the so-called media multiplier effect (Smith 1997, Weser 1997, Billett 2002).

The means to achieve this is generally recognised as creativity (what brands go to creative communication agencies for), media strategy and implementation (the contribution of the media agency) and a single, media neutral, powerful idea, which is a product of research plus inspiration (often contributed by the 'above the line' advertising agency). An example of this is the SEEBOARD Energy idea: Where does it all come from? This playful idea was used in a variety of creative and humorous treatments. Another is the idea 'Mini adventure' which was successfully used by BMW to launch the new Mini, leading to a variety of executions in each of which there is a very short story involving Mini saving the world.

According to Nigel Howlett, global strategy director of OgilvyOne, every successful integrated campaign at Ogilvy has depended on a media neutral idea. The value of such an organising or governing idea is that it provides a creative frame for multiple intelligences to produce a wide variety of communications content and format that share a common identity, achieving the creative objectives of wholeness outlined above.

In practice, it seems that great communications arise out of an interplay between at least two governing ideas, and often four or five: principally the brand essence, the core positioning, long-term or sustained idea that drives the brand's vision of value to customers, the essence of the attraction at each customer community has for the brand, and the seasonal, media neutral, creative idea, which keeps its communication youthful and relevant. For example, IBM's worldwide communications had been driven for a number of years by the idea 'e-business' in partnership with its BrandPrint (the brand essence and values) before it recently adopted the new business concept 'on demand' that was launched in 2002 to drive communications and strategy. However, individual communication projects, such as the IBM City of London campaigns of 2001 and 2002, or its global developerWorks communication project, used media neutral creative ideas (e.g. 'a wakeup call') to facilitate communicating the big idea in ways that were fresh and appropriate for the customer community or communities.

Just as most music is based on polyphony and its interplay of melody and counterpoint, and most works of imaginative literature on multiple plots and characters, so creative marketing communication also arises out of the drama between ideas. Indeed, Ehrenzweig (1967), an authority on art and creativity, comments that: 'All artistic structure is essentially "polyphonic": it evolves not in a single line of thought, but in several superimposed strands at once'.

Going Integrated: making it happen

Research at the Centre for Integrated Marketing has identified a number of factors that lead towards Integrated Marketing success. While these can be represented as a simple Gnatt chart and project programme, it is also useful to see them as a network of stepping-stones or actions, shown in Figure 7.3 in the network diagram, which also shows the primary activity flows. Each 'stepping stone' represents a major initiative for senior leaders to implement. Marketing manage-

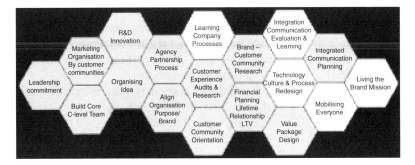

Figure 7.3   Implementing Integrated Marketing: the action network
Source: The authors.

ment does not need to be responsible for most of these, but they have a significant opportunity to make a difference and the responsibility to ensure harmonised action.

As the diagram shows the action areas are interdependent. Each of them also includes a further detailed set of actions. However, the case studies suggest that the action network is also relatively fluid and creative. For example, leaders initiate the 18 potential actions in different sequences or priorities. They might also give relatively more or less weight to different actions depending on the brand situation, and they might initiate change from more than one place or connect together existing initiatives. For example, one leader might achieve a marketing revolution by transforming the structure and working of the marketing function (as we found with IBM (Jenkinson and Sain 2003h)) while another might achieve dramatic results through its 'organising idea' (e.g. i2 or The Automobile Association) while another might give priority to technology, culture and process design (as with Centrica), based on either strategic opportunity or current weakness. For example, one company may already have a very strong alignment behind the organisational purpose and the brand while another may have very high quality technology. In each situation, leaders focus on relative priorities and/or factors that are easier to implement.

Almost any of these areas can serve as a beginning point for effective change and value creation. However the maximum benefit will be achieved when organisations broadly work from left to right across the network of actions, avoiding independent (fragmented) initiatives in favour of a connected approach, as in the case of SEEBOARD Energy. For example, a workforce motivated by an ideal is more likely to achieve the other objectives than one operating by rule and objectives.

Where existing initiatives already take place – for example a company may already be working on learning processes (Senge 1992, Revans 1998) – then the aim would be to connect them with a minimum level of disruption and the maximum level of affirmation possible in order to maintain motivation and progress to date.

Space does not allow a detailed explanation, but the key point is that transformation is possible, benefits from senior marketers adopting their expanded role, and in the case of SEEBOARD Energy led to very significant results in less than 12 months. All of our research partners have managed to achieve major results in at least the areas in which they primarily focus in such a period.

1. Leadership Commitment: to make a beginning and to sustain the process of change.
2. Build Core C-Level Team: the senior team need to contract to take responsibility for one or more elements within an interlocking set of objectives and organisation change projects.
3. Organising Idea: championing the key organising idea/ideas that shape the business is the key role of leadership.
4. Align Organisation Purpose/Brand: ensure that the organisation is designed and motivated to reflect its mission, purpose and brand promise.
5. Customer Community Orientation: design the organisation so that it is tailored to deliver value to its different customer communities.
6. Organise marketing by customer communities: This fuels the process of change and is a seed act that can produce a thousand blooms.
7. Agency Partnership Process: rationalise the agency relationships into a single team partnership.
8. Brand-Customer Community Research: the core attributes of the brand signature, the primary customer communities and their archetypal members.
9. Customer Experience Audits and Research: by community across all key Touchpoints.
10. Learning Company Processes: a pre-requisite for a sharing and therefore integrated business.
11. Financial Planning, Lifetime Relationship and Lifetime Value: Integrated Marketing is a hard-headed discipline, that recognises both a necessity to make profits and the opportunity of maximising lifetime value.
12. Value Package Design: develop distinctive, high value propositions for the different financial segments within each community.

13. R&D Innovation: Integrated Marketing does not accept that it is necessary to provide me-too solutions. Genuine differentiation and added value is the only certain way to survive in a competitive world.
14. Technology, Culture and Process Redesign: the means to deliver.
15. Integrated Communications Planning: media neutral planning and creative ideas.
16. Integrated Communication Evaluation and Learning: a common currency for all Touchpoint/media communication and an evaluation method that accumulates data and knowledge for econometric modelling and learning.
17. Mobilising Everyone: involving, inspiring and directing everyone.
18. Living the Brand Mission: a goal, but also an ongoing process to nurture and manage.

Conclusion

Integrated Marketing is here to stay and to develop. The name might change, but the concept will not. It is a way of thinking and operating that enhances value for customers, employees and the organisation and leads to the resolution of many of the current frustrations within the marketing industry. Marketing now has a new responsibility, and so do those in the business of marketing communications.

Ensure that your organisation/brand is creatively aligned to its fundamental truth through a coherent, service-based ideal and vision of achievable success. Ensure congruence of brand and culture, of leadership and people aspiration, of vision and of practice. Organise the business in processes to deliver value and communication to customers, not into silos. Practice genuine partnership between clients and agencies and agency teams, building trust and understanding.

There are huge business opportunities to follow.

References

Billett, J. (2002) *Hard edged consumer issues and hard nosed media solutions*, CIM Publications, Maidenhead.

Christopher, M., Payne, A. and Ballantyne, D. (1991) *Relationship Marketing*, Butterworth Heinemann, Oxford.

Ehrenzweig, A. (1967) *The Hidden Order of Art*, Phoenix Press, London.

Ghoshal, S. and Bartlett, C.A. (1998) *The Individualised Corporation*, Heinemann, London.

Jenkinson, A. (1994) Beyond Segmentation, *Journal of Targeting, Marketing and Analysis for Measurement*, Vol. 3 (No. 1), pp. 60–72.

Jenkinson, A. (1995) *Valuing Your Customers*, McGraw Hill, London.

The following case materials (written by Jenkinson and Sain) concerning integrated marketing can be obtained from the Centre for Integrated Marketing, at http://www.integratedmarketing.org.uk/

- AOL, redefining marcoms (2002a)
- SEEBOARD Energy, Integrated Marketing transforms the brand fortunes (2002b)
- i2 shows the way (2002c)
- Amazon: bonding customers with integrated service (2003d)
- Sainsbury's Little Ones programme (2003e)
- The Automobile Association: how a big idea put the AA back together (2003f)
- Harley Davidson, organisation led Integrated Marketing (2003g)
- IBM, a new model for IMC (2003h)

Kitchen, P.J. (2003a) *The Future of Marketing: Critical 21st Century Perspectives*, Palgrave–Macmillan, Basingstoke.
Kitchen, P.J. (2003b) *The Rhetoric and Reality of Marketing: An International Managerial Approach*, Palgrave–Macmillan, Basingstoke.
Kunde, J. (2002) *Unique Now… or Never: the Brand Is the Company Driver in the New Value Economy*, Financial Times/Prentice Hall: London.
Lauterborn, B. (1990) *New marketing litany: four p's passe; c-words take over*, Advertising Age, Midwest Region Edition, Chicago, 1 Oct., Vol. 61, Issue 41, p. 26.
Lievegoed, B. (1991) *Managing The Developing Organisation*, Blackwell: London.
Normann, R. (1984) *Service Management*, John Wiley & Sons, Chichester.
Reichheld, F.F. (1996) *The Loyalty Effect*, Harvard Business School Press: Harvard, Mass.
Revans, R. (1998) *ABC of Action Learning*, Lemos & Crane, London.
Schneider, B. (1980) The Service Organisation: climate is crucial, *Organisational Dynamics*, Autumn Vol. 2, 1, American Management Association pp. 52–65.
Schultz, D.E. and Kitchen, P.J. (2000) *Communicating Globally: An Integrated Marketing Approach*, Macmillan Press Ltd, London, p. 3, 32, 62, 188.
Schultz, Don E. (2002) *The Future of Branding in Residential Utilities*, Datamonitor, London.
Senge, P.M. (1992) *The Fifth Discipline*, Century Business, London.
Smith, A. (1997) *Integrated marketing communications starts with print plus television*, Proceedings of ESOMAR Latin American Conference, Rio do Janeiro, pp. 237–249
Teerlink, R. and Ozley, L. (2000) *More Than A Motorcycle*, Harvard Business School Press: Harvard, Mass.
Weser, A. (1997) *Advertising increases market shares and media mix achieves most: The proof: WerbeWert 97*, European Society for Opinion and Marketing Research, Lisbon.
Whiteley, C. (1991) *The Customer Driven Company*, Century Business, London.

8
Beyond Relationship Marketing

Charles Chien and Luiz Moutinho

Introduction

Let's move the boundaries forward. We've all heard of relationship marketing. Here we attempt to move beyond the known, the tried, the tested. We want to move the argument to a higher plane. As usual 'height' is a matter of intellectual curiosity and managerial practice. Let's set forth on our journey … .

This essay has a number of topics to discuss:

1. It develops a relational view of the market by dissecting patterns of reciprocal exchanges.
2. It follows a platform derived from evolutionary social psychology as a backdrop for participatory exchange and the study of dyadic norms.
3. It takes the view of a market as a signifier of a social system in which attitudinal directions can be detected.

With these antecedents in mind, we intend to provoke 'mental stretching and simulations' by projecting conceptualisations beyond modern contractual relations. We emphasise degrees of deviation and reciprocal dispersion surrounding relationships which should be based on reciprocal solidarity! We comment on the changing span of expectations experienced by relationship parties, their small (getting smaller) zones of tolerance, and the sub-segment psychological gain surplus. With these conceptual foundations, we attempt to analyse how the process of facilitation of commonalities between relationship parties leads to utility maximisation.

Undoubtedly, marketing reality is replete with poor examples of market relationships. Our perspective is that one of the core elements of exchange is based on the ultimate goal designed to bring future outcomes (goals) into the present (current assessment). This perspective then evolves into the formation of long-term customer franchises. Moreover, we believe businesses do want to establish long-term sustainable preferences in their customer, preferably comprised of non-artificial relational facets. The context here is building successful relationships, as in any other strand of life.

Do you recall the research focus and furore on customer service in the early '80s, total quality management in the late '80s, and service quality in the '90s? Yet, in the 21st century market success is neither defined by innovative products nor indeed by customer satisfaction. Instead, market success is more likely to be based on profitable market relationships (Day 2000). Marketing is evolving toward a relationship orientation, perceived as retained connections to constellate value between buyers and sellers. The value of the relationship between buyers and sellers is arguably the basic constituent of true market value (Achrol and Kotler 1999). The stronger the relationship, the better the market success; thus, market relationships are increasingly viewed as competitive assets of a firm by managers (Deshpande 1999, Gruen et al. 2000). A current market portrait is changing from a segmentation viewpoint toward a network perspective (Achrol and Kotler 1999, Day and Montgomery 1999). Relationship marketing is now seen as the major shift in marketing thought and practice (Gummesson 1999, Sheth and Parvatiyar 2002, Webster 1992).

Yet, relationship marketing (RM) is a 'new-old' concept (Berry 1995). Its tenets have been around for some time. Terms, such as database marketing, loyalty programs, and others, are cited as synonyms to RM; but the underlying principles of RM are really indistinguishable from the principles of marketing (Baker 1998, Fournier et al. 1998). Yet even the verb 'relationship' will become less relevant, when it matures to be an essential and basic principle of marketing (Palmer 2002). Somehow, though, knowledge regarding the specific content of customer relationships is sparse and disparate. So we will discuss here concepts of relationship marketing. Our argument is grounded in:

1. Drawing upon up-stream conceptualisations for a theoretical hub (Siew 1985, Bagozzi 1979).
2. Revisiting the classic conceptual works of relationship marketing (Dwyer et al. 1987, Macneil 1980).
3. Borrowing from the sister disciplines of psychology and evolutionary psychology to attempt to explain relationship behaviour.

4. Application of a formal language definition system (Hunt 1991, Teas and Palan 1997).

Non-presentiation

One of the distinct natures of relationship marketing concerns perception of future time. Attitude relating to time is an important aspect of expectation in a relationship. There would be no stage for a 'relationship' to play a role in a marketing exchange, if there is no need for time continuity between two parties. Not all marketing relationships equate to relationship marketing (Sheth and Parvatiyar 2002). Macneil (1980) explains this distinction by categorising market relations into three types: discrete transaction, modern relations, and primitive relations. The differences originate from dissimilar assumptions underlying future orientations of discrete and relational exchanges. A discrete exchange is one in which no relation exists between the parties apart from the simple exchange of goods (sounds like much of current political marketing). In discrete exchanges, the future is treated as a controllable factor in that future risk is calculated into a present cost. The ultimate goal of parties concerning a discrete transaction is to bring all the future relating to it into the *present* or in a rare but precise word used by Macneil (1980), into the *'presentiate'*. The parties can then deal with the future. This is what the neoclassical microeconomic model regularly purports to do with the future as if it were in the present. The properties of 'presentiation' of a discrete exchange would lead to very complete and specific planning without flexible future projecting. And the focus of the planning is on the substance of the exchange.

However, only absolutely binding planning under the assumption of pure rationality can do presentiation, as shown on the left-hand side of Figure 8.1. In primitive relations, the future is viewed as open to what happens, never in a sense of presentiation. The incompleteness and lack of precision in rational planning for the future *leave the future where it is*. Presentiation thus does not occur in primitive exchange relations. The future can only be prepared for, never conquered. Therefore, in primitive relations, time can be viewed as nonpresentiation, as shown on the right-hand side of Figure 8.1. In primitive relations, future projecting is embedded with unspecified flexibility. So rational planning takes place in vain; intuitive decisions are taken on the basis of experience and accumulated judgment. Thus the nature of nonpresentiation is emphasised. In modern exchange

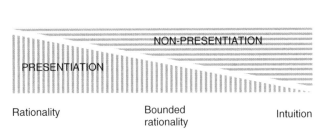

Discrete transaction	Modern relations	Primitive relations

Rationality	Bounded rationality	Intuition

Figure 8.1   Nonpresentiation and presentation

relations, future projection is more specifically prepared for but not managed as in the discrete type approach. It is a mixed type of relations that contain both natures of presentation and nonpresentation, as shown in Figure 8.1. Decisions are made on the basis of 'good enough' rationality. In fact, this leads to one of the most popular relations in our contemporary business society, in which the basis for future collaboration may be supported by some degree of explicit planning and implicit assumptions – trust.

For example, a road accident may cause a serious traffic jam, an event that obviously may affect an obligation of a delivery to be on time to a destination. In an ideal discrete transaction that contingency would be precisely planned for, and moreover, the risk of its happening would have been taken into account in a pricing agreement. Nevertheless, in an earthquake, for instance, instead of a road accident, presentiate contract, agreed by both parties, provides no solutions to such uncertainty. If the parties had thought at all beyond the ever-present, they would have adapted a nonpresentation mode of strategy in order to deal with the problem with the whole range of personal (parties') resources including community support available for hard times. The ultimate goal of the parties to a relational exchange is to bring all the future related to it into the *whole person* who has committed to provide the substance as well as exchange process of substance. The whole person is the focus in the process of relational exchange with tacit assumptions of sharing benefits and burdens (Dwyer et al. 1987).

Projection is an affirmation of the power of human will to affect the future. Nevertheless, the future can only be adapted for and not controlled in day-to-day operations (Macneil 1980). Sensibility of the future causes people to cope with its uncertainty through cooperative exchange relations. In a risk situation, such tendencies towards a relationship can best be understood by borrowing the notion of evolutionary social psychology (Buss and Kenrick 1998). They believe, in coping with future uncertainty, that cooperative relations is an important survival strategy that we inherit ancestrally. Their example scenario is: in an ancestral environment in which meat is scarce and high in variance, a hunter might go for days without catching an animal, but when he or she does, there might be a sudden bounty. Meat spoils without refrigeration, and there is only so much meat a person can consume. If hunter A gives hunter B a share of meat when A is luckily successful and vice versa, then they both benefit. The costs of providing a benefit to another are lower than the benefits received. Also, the total possibility of hunter A and B's success is certainly greater than the possibility of each individual success. The relationships formed between hunter A and B explain the flexibility nature of non-presentation, and is an innate survival strategy to cope with the uncertainty of the future. Non-presentation is thus a mode of flexible future projecting.

The managerial implications of this are two-fold. Relationship marketing involves developing offerings that are able to flexibly solve customer's current *and* future needs and wants. A company with a rigid inflexible service policy – and there are many – would find it very difficult to develop reciprocal relations with their customers. For example, in a bill payment of a mobile phone, a disconnect policy was deployed to an overdue client who had been with the company for three years with a good record. The client paid the bill through an ATM, but payment was short of £2 by mistake. The company insisted that the full bill amount be paid and a reconnection charge because that is how the computer system worked to carry out the policy. This client (and likely many others) left the service forever! Obviously, strategies concerning characteristics of flexible non-presentation could be a window for companies to develop and use relational touch-point services with customers. Certainly, empowerment programmes in training service employees to perform relational touch-point services is crucial. There may well be lessons here for all those services with automated response services, most of which do annoy and irritate customers (perhaps deliberately). Human personnel with a knowledge of how things really work is always better than the best automated computer.

If marketing offerings are completely planned; unexpected outcomes are not allowed, there are no incentives for customers to move forward from transactional types of purchasing to relational types of buying. The elasticity of such offerings impacting on repurchasing behaviour could be low. For example, in bygone days, a grocery store's strategy of relational pricing or preferential treatment on a non-routine basis could possibly increase the elasticity of relational offerings. Today, Dell Computer, with advances in Internet technology, can and does utilise its advantage of economies of scale to customise on-line computer orders for global corporate customers, and is extending this through business-to-customer channels. In another example, a Lexus executive stated: 'Our company's aim goes beyond satisfying the customer. Our aim is to delight the customer'. Yet, 'satisfaction' and 'delight' may be mere rhetorical flourishes if no attempt is made to build real relationships that transcend individual transactions.

Evidently, both transactional and relational marketing activities could create satisfied customers, but only relational marketing efforts offer the potential to go beyond expected satisfactions and deliver potentially delighting experiences. Understanding that complaints represent a deviation from the norm for customers also represents an opportunity to develop improved touch-point services and potentially leverage better relationships with customers . For example, 3M strongly encourage customers to submit complaints and suggestions. As a result, over two-thirds of its product-improvement ideas come from these relational assets. The customer's experience of customer-complaint could be also a strategic window for a company to more effectively develop long-term franchises with customers.

Reciprocal dispersion

Reciprocal dispersion is a framework designed to gauge the degree of relationship intensity. The larger the dispersion, the greater the relationship intensity, and vice versa. Reciprocal dispersion is explained as the degree of deviation (illustrated as the fat arrows stand within upper and lower lines of limit in Figure 8.2) that the partner's perception (demonstrated as the oscillated experience line in Figure 8.2) fluctuates, as exchange experiences go along, within the span of expectation (shown as upper and lower lines of expectation limit in Figure 8.2). The span of expectation governs what is accepted and unaccepted for exchange functions; those within are acceptable, those outside are unacceptable. It also can be perceived as a zone of tolerance for good and bad relations. The greater the zone of tolerance, the closer the relationship. In a discrete transaction, there is no span of expectation, in which the upper line of limit joins the lower line, and the graph line of experienced perception meets the line of expectation, all lines converge into one baseline as illustrated as a laid arrow in Figure 8.2. The zero degree of deviation, sketched as the baseline arrow, reflects the nature of discrete transactions that allow no space for unexpected outcomes. If unexpected outcomes of experiencing perceptions are tolerated, some degree of trust would be needed; then reciprocal dispersion is created. Furthermore, on the basis of trust, cooperative dispersion reflecting greater span of tolerated expectation can be achieved in a process of relationship establishment. Although not every experience instance would reach the upper or lower limits of tolerance, once it is reached, it is still accepted. Finally, a committed relationship mirrors the highest degree of dispersion, as shown in Figure 8.2.

Trust and commitment have emerged as building blocks of relationship marketing theory, and are understood as focal constructs of effective relationships (Anderson and Barton 1992, Ganesan 1994, Garbarino and Johnson 1999). The higher level of trust and commitment that help govern exchange characterise relational exchange; and conversely, the lower level of such relational attributes reflect discrete transactions (Morgan and Hunt 1994). However, as research interest grows in relationship marketing, the more evidence unfolds indicating that there are well-recognised elements of trust and commitment in

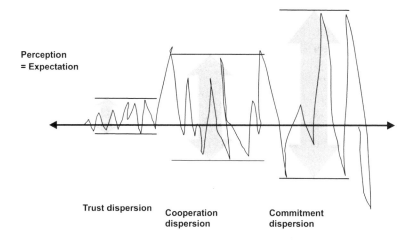

Perception
= Expectation

Trust dispersion · Cooperation dispersion · Commitment dispersion

Figure 8.2 Reciprocal dispersion

exchange relationships. For example, a dark side of long-term relationships has been documented (Grayson and Ambler 1999, Moorman et al. 1992, Reinartz and Kumar 2000) that:

1. trust does not have any effect on long-term service usage
2. trust is only important only in the early stage of relationships
3. higher levels of commitment can even reduce service usage in knowledge-based exchanges, such as advertising services.

In Figure 8.2, trust, sketched as a smaller span of dispersion, is viewed as a basic reliant pattern of reciprocal solidarity that governs what is correct for exchange functions. Thus, in an industrial purchasing context, trust operates as an 'order qualifier', not an 'order winner'. In fact, price and reliable delivery actually make the sale (Doney and Cannon 1997), not trust. In a study of multidimensional relationships, high levels of trust are reported in both discrete and relational types of exchange, in the 'basic buying – selling' and in the 'customer is king' area (Cannon and Perreault 1999). Thus, trust is a basic reliant pattern and a prerequisite but not sufficient condition for a relational exchange. On the other hand, the mechanism of commitment is designed to generate high covariance between two partners' variances, such as the stated example of hunters A and B. This is particularly critical in a high uncertainty context. But in a market exchange, the majority of relational exchanges would not need to reach that high degree of tolerance, as is needed for example in marriage. In most cases, the cooperative pattern of reciprocal exchange could become strong enough for a business relationship to operate in a median degree of uncertainty.

By strategically enlarging the reciprocal dispersion, the company could position itself as a highly committed marketer to its customers' relationships. L.L. Bean, which runs a mail order and Internet catalogue business in clothing and equipment, has carefully blended its marketing programmes to deliver this relational position. To its customers, it offers its commitment: 100 per cent guarantee –

All of our products are guaranteed to give 100% satisfaction in every way. Return anything purchased from us at any time if it proves otherwise. We will replace it, refund your purchase price or credit your credit card, as you wish. We do not want you to have anything from L.L. Bean that is not completely satisfactory. (Courtesy L.L. Bean 1998)

This position sells L.L. Bean's relationships to its customers. The company commits to its served market. The higher degree of reciprocal dispersion leads to the higher propensity to market the company's relationships to its customers.

Personification

Personification is a concept contrasting to the popular concept of personalisation that is most emphasised by customer relationship management, CRM. The personalisation programme of CRM has been running into the classic marketing mistake, the metaphor of 'captain' style of marketing activities. Customers are fish; the duty of captain is to catch (build relationships with) the fish. The fish (customer) has to run away. Peppers and Rogers (1993) proclaim that once a relationship is the marketing goal, an important step is to identify individual customers and to gather information about them, which is the foundational concept of personalisation (Peppers and Rogers 1997). Personalisation is defined to be any form of customisation that occurs because of specific recognition of a given customer (Kalyanam and McIntyre 2002). Personalisation can be categorised as follows:

1. *customisation*, the system's ability to customise items by allowing individual users to set their own preferences;
2. *individualisation,* the system's ability to customise itself to the user based on the user's exhibited behaviour; and
3. *group characterisation*, the system's ability to customise itself to the user based on the preferences of other users with similar interests.

The collection of data for personalisation forces the marketer to decide how this information is to be used, particularly regarding access to it, thus the basic decision about privacy is made prior to, and when the marketer collects information about the individual and stores it. Dot.com retailers that offer product customisation have been the group hit the hardest by the stock market. In fact, 78 per cent of these firms were trading their stock at less than $1 (Mahajan et al. 2002). Product customisation alone does not help an online retailer perform well (Mahajan et al. 2002). The more the CRM endeavour, the less customer relationships seem to be built. The explanation could be derived from Macneil's (1980) concept of whole person in a relational exchange. In a discrete transaction, substance of exchange is the focal point, whereas, in a relational exchange, the focal point of exchange is more broadly generalised on the substance provider. The provider's commitment stands for his/her product quality and service guarantee. The provider, as a whole person, signifies a cue of trust for buyer. Berry's (1986) archetype of relationship marketing is the interaction between a grandpa grocery store and its community. The owner, as a whole person, is a clear human identity for customers naturally to project their relational emotion to. But this simple nature of interaction becomes extremely difficult for a large organisation to exercise. The identity, as a base for customer to project his/her emotion to, is gone. The focus of a relationship strategy is on the company's offerings, not on a customer's private profile. A programme based on a relational personification system could assist the company to act as a whole person and to design relational touch point interfaces. The secret to build a customer relationship is personification not personalisation.

A definitional framework

Ironically, despite convergent research interests on relationships, the relationship concept is hindered by its ambiguities. One important fact is that the term relationship is part of our common language (Berscheid and Peplau 1983). Thus, using the word 'relationship' often carries an assumption that the meaning of the word is obvious. Another source in this vague domain is that not only does the term carry a wide variety of meanings among theorists (Bagozzi 1995); but often these meanings have not been specified (Reis, Collins and Berscheid 2000). The term, *relationship*, often appears in titles, without definition.

In the following sections, we specify a formal language system[1] that was proposed by Hunt (1991) and Teas and Palan (1997) to delineate the precision necessary for the development of theoretically meaningful concepts of exchange relationships.

Beginning with a fundamental foundation of the exchange concept, we specify the derived term[2] – utility. The starting point for wanting to establish exchanges with others is the utilitarian benefits of living. The human desire to maximise selfish benefits and yet maintain social acceptance with others are underlying utilitarian behaviours (Bagozzi 1995). Thus, using the two primitive terms, 'want(s)' and 'benefit(s)', the concept of utility and exchange utility are defined as follows:

1. *Utility:* The want of perceived benefits.
2. *Exchange Utility:* The exchange of wants for perceived benefits among two or more parties.

Exchange utility in a discrete transaction, as Macneil (1980, p. 14) noted, is the 'immediate gains each party sees in exchanging' with no further planning anticipated. It is carefully measured and specified and to bring all the future benefits and burdens into the present, with an emphasis on the divisiveness and selfishness inherent in exchange (Dwyer et al. 1987). However, some of the elements of exchange, instead of occurring immediately, will only occur in the future, such as the previous example of hunters A and B. This awareness of future regularly shifts people's orientation from autonomy to relatedness, and cause people do things differently (Hodgins, Koestner and Duncan 1996). When these behaviours relate to exchange, it is projected forward in time. As people preparing for the future, utilitarian benefits of living will not be maximised without projecting benefits into the future.

Future anticipation can substantially affect people's adaptation of different modes of behaviour (Lemon et al. 2002, Taylor et al. 1998). For example, Taylor and Pham (1996) found that when an exchange party engages in future anticipation, the likelihood of current behaviour that will be consistent with futuristic mental simulations is significantly increased. Consumers are forward-looking when they make the decision to continue or discontinue an exchange relationship (Lemon et al. 2002). The term 'projecting' is a concept that Macneil (1980) used to define relational exchange. Without 'projecting' the relating mechanism will be all presentation in that the future can be dealt with as if it were in the present, in other words, discrete (Macniel 1980). Using other primitive terms 'move', 'future', and def2, the definition for a concept of projection or, to use a rare word, projectability, is derived as follows:

3. *Projectability:* The process of moving exchange utilities forward into the future.

The concept of projectability is comparable but different from long-term orientation. Long-term orientation focuses on the perception of interdependence of outcomes, in which partners' joint outcomes are expected to benefit both parties in the long run (Ganesan 1994, Kelley and Thibaut 1978). This concept is grounded more on the governance perspective of relationships in terms of time span. Projectability, nevertheless, emphasises a look forward into the future, which reflects more on the viewpoint of relating rather than of governance.[3] The effect of time span on relationship building could be neutral (Reinartz and Kumar 2000). But without projectability, there will not be an opportunity for relationship development. In the conceptual domain of projectability, long-term orientation is preferred but not necessary. Projectability is also similar but unequal to the concept of future intentions in that assessment of consumers' potential to remain with or leave an organisation is emphasised (Garbarino and Johnson 1999). The idea of future intention is an affirmation of human-will affecting the future. It is parallel to the notion of presentiation that the future can be dealt with as if it were in the present. Nevertheless, the future can only be adapted for, not controlled, in day-to-day operations (Macneil 1980). As discussed before, non-presentiation is one distinct characteristic of a relationship.

Sensibility of the future causes people to cope with the uncertainty of future exchanges through cooperative relatedness and social legitimacy. Projectability emanates from utility reflecting a higher level of abstraction. It could only be functional when combining with, at least, some degree of governance mechanism in a social matrix that regulates exchanges. Research in transactional cost analysis (TCA), (Williamson 1985) has proposed market, relationalism, and hierarchies as three different forms of governance mechanism. In relational exchange, partners rely on either primitive or modern relational contracts to govern the exchange process. In primitive contractual relations, such as kinship and friendship, custom, status etiquette, and habit are sources of exchange solidarity providing a sense of what is right and proper (Macneil 1980). In modern contractual relations, such as sophisticated networks of specialisation among businesses, sources of exchange solidarity are explicit or implicit management policies and exchange agreements (Dwyer et al. 1987). Exchange solidarity, a regulation of exchange behaviour to ensure exchange function, is derived from the concept of the governance perspective of relationship. Thus, the derived term of exchange solidarity would be defined by using primitive terms – 'source(s)', 'correct', 'govern', and the common derived term – 'exchange function', as follows:

4. *Exchange Solidarity*: Sources that govern what is correct for exchange functions.

Furthermore, it is helpful to divide exchange solidarity into two classes, internal and external. Sources of solidarity are not only built from internal norms of shared beliefs between exchange partners, but are also grounded on external norms that are the second-order institutions embedded within social justifications (Gouldner 1960, Macneil 1980). Institutional theory (Fennel and Alexander 1987, Hirsch 1975, Meyer and Scott 1983) suggests that institutional environments impose pressures on social actors to justify their activities or outputs. These pressures motivate social actors to increase their legitimacy in order to appear in agreement with the prevailing norms, standards of proper conduct, rules, beliefs or expectations of external constituents. Thus, primitive terms of 'belief', 'individual', 'social', 'justification' and def4 are used to defined the derived concepts of internal exchange solidarity and external exchange solidarity as follows:

5. *Internal Exchange Solidarity*: Individual belief in exchange solidarity
6. *External Exchange Solidarity:* Social justification of exchange solidarity

Relationships occur for the purpose of pursuing common or mutually beneficial goals or interests (Wilson 1995). As Gouldner (1960) stated – there is altruism in egoism, but it is only possible through perceived reciprocity. A mechanism of reciprocity leverages selfish utility into the future, and also reduces uncertainty. As a matter of fact, we all live under rules of reciprocity that people will innately seek to help those who help them – a tenet dating back at least 2000 years (Cacioppo et al. 2000). It is a pattern of exchange through which mutually beneficial goals, brought about by the division of labor, are realised.

Beyond reciprocity as a pattern of exchange and beyond folk beliefs about reciprocity as a fact of life, there is another element: a generalised norm of legitimacy that justifies certain accepted actions and institutionalises dyadic reciprocity into a social system (Gouldner 1960). The establishment of relationships for the purpose of increasing legitimacy can originate from a social actor's motives to demonstrate or improve its reputation, image, prestige or congruence with the prevailing norms in its social environment (Oliver 1990). Reciprocity is a dyadic norm, a social significant exchange solidarity between two parties. On the other hand, legitimacy is a triadic contract, a social acceptance of exchange solidarity among more than three associated persons. In a relationship, as Gouldner (1960) posited, 'the sentiment of gratitude joints forces with the sentiment of rectitude and adds a safety-margin in the motivation to conformity [of the relational exchange]' (p. 68). Therefore, using these definitions and the primitive terms – 'mutual', 'pattern', 'gratify', and 'acceptance', reciprocity and legitimacy can be defined as follows:

7. *Reciprocity:* The mutually gratifying pattern of internal exchange solidarity
8. *Legitimacy:* The degree of acceptance for external exchange solidarity

Finally, the concept of exchange relationship can use the primitive terms 'linkage' and 'process' and def7&8, in conjunction with def3 to be posited as:

9. *Relationship Exchange*: The linkage between parties as to reciprocity and legitimacy in the projectability process.
10. *Relationship Marketing*: marketing activities designed toward establishing, developing, and maintaining a *relationship exchange*.

Syntactically, the formal language of exchange relationship can be presented as shown in Figure 8.3.

In a business sense, the utility continuum is the basic selfishness nature of human focusing on the time projection of survival. Nevertheless, as time is prolonged, uncertainty increases. It is impossible to function under such uncertainty without social collaboration. Although human beings are opportunistic creatures, they are inevitably limited by norms of exchange solidarity. The exchange solidarity is the social nature that leads to interaction and cooperation with primary and secondary social groups. Within a primary group, internal exchange solidarity regulates the exchange parties' behaviours,

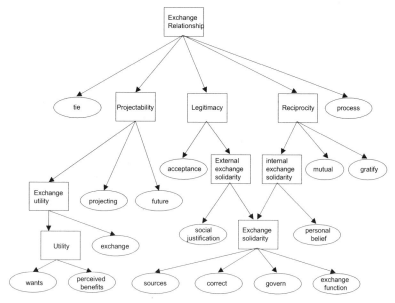

Figure 8.3   Formal language definition of exchange relationship
Source: The authors.

such as trust, cooperativeness and commitment. In a secondary group, external exchange solidarity governs the two parties' interrelationship, such as reputation and recognition, or institutional trust, a term introduced by Zucker (1986). When a customer intends to buy a recreational vehicle, utility concerns, such as product benefits and price, will be the focal point. Yet as concerns for future maintenance are thought of, they complicate purchasing decisions. Consumers will then look for clues of reciprocal trustworthiness in the salesperson and the legitimacy of the corporate image of the car dealer. Borrowing from psychology and evolutionary social psychology perspective, such relationship behaviour is much the same as our ancestors' in the Stone Age (Buss and Kenrick 1998, Cacioppo et al. 2000, Reis et al. 2000). Human exchange relationship behaviours today are well-preserved fossils (Buss and Kenrick 1998) incorporating an ancestral survival strategy of utility, reciprocity, legitimacy, and projectability. The four characteristics of relationship marketing are illustrated in Figure 8.4, and will be discussed below.

Utility and projectability

The starting point for a need to exchange with others is the utilitarian benefit of living.

Consumer desire to maximise selfish benefits and to create and maintain social solidarity with other participants are underlying

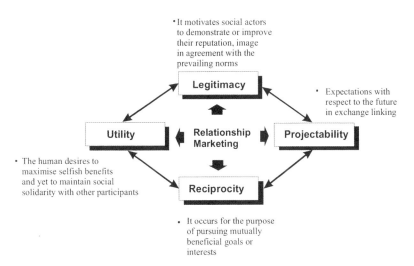

Figure 8.4   The four characteristics of relationship marketing

utilitarian behaviours (Bagozzi 1995). It is the fundamental nature of choice-induced exchange and all participatory exchange that benefit is only possible when there is possible economic or/and psychic gain-surplus resulting from exchange (Macneil 1980). Utilitarian behaviour in relationships involves calculation, comparison, and awareness of the exchange (Anderson and Narus 1984, Oliver 1990). The characteristics of measurement and specificity in relational exchange reveal the significant attention paid to measuring, specifying, and quantifying all aspects of performance, including psychic and future benefits (Dwyer et al. 1987, Wilson 1995).

The utilitarian benefit of living will not be maximised without projecting this benefit into the future. Projectability is the characteristic that invariably does appear in relations, must appear if relations are to continue, and consequently ought to appear as long as their continuance is valued (Macneil 1980). Projectability can be seen as the expectations respecting the future in the exchange linkage. Projectability in a relationship consists of the notions of (1) planning (Macneil 1980), (2) adaptation (Wilson 1995), (3) preservation of the relation (Macneil 1980), (4) expectations for the relation (Dwyer, Schurr, and Oh 1987), and (5) timing of exchange (Dwyer, Schurr and Oh 1987, Macneil 1980).

Reciprocity and legitimacy

Exchange, as a social meaning, is a great revolutionary discovery by our ancestors. It is built on an infrastructure of promise. Reciprocity is a dyadic norm, equating to social significant exchange solidarity between two parties. Legitimacy, here, is a triadic contract, social acceptance of exchange solidarity among three associated persons.

Relationships occur for the purpose of pursuing common or mutually beneficial goals or interests. A mechanism of reciprocity leverages selfish utility into the future, and also reduces future uncertainty.

Morgan and Hunt (1994) theorised with empirical support that commitment and trust are key mediating variables for a successful relationship. It is helpful to treat the constructs of commitment and trust as intermediate level concepts so as to explain reciprocity as a higher-level concept, and also to illustrate lower-level concepts such as role integrity (Macneil 1979), interpersonal emotions (Bagozzi 1995), and mutual goals (Wilson 1995).

Beyond reciprocity as a pattern of exchange and beyond folk beliefs about reciprocity as a fact of life, there is another element: a generalised norm of legitimacy that justifies certain accepted actions and institutionalises the dyadic reciprocity into a social system (Gouldner 1960). Institutional theory (Fennel and Alexander 1978, Hirsch 1975, Meyer and Scott 1983) suggests that institutional environments impose pressures on social actors to justify their activities or outputs. These pressures motivate social actors to increase their legitimacy in order to appear in agreement with prevailing norms, standards of proper conduct, rules, beliefs or expectations of external constituents. The establishment of relationships for purposes of increasing legitimacy can originate from a social actor's motives to demonstrate or improve its reputation, image, prestige or congruence with the prevailing norms in its social environment (Oliver 1990).

Empirical evidence

How are the associations among utility, reciprocity, legitimacy and projectability (URLeP) measured? Bharadwaj et al. (1993) suggest that the greater the intangibility of a service, the greater the importance of a legitimate image as a source of information for consumer to assess their purchasing risks. Wilson (1995) postulated the reputation variable is part of the very first phase of relationship development process. Day and Montgomery (1999) reveal that a decade of research progress in brand equity has shown that 'strong brands are valuable to the firms that own them because they represent the history of past relationships and the promise of future ones'. In a relatedness experience, legitimacy is postulated as the first tendency of attitude directions among URLeP (Chien and Moutinho 2000). An accepted legitimate image could affect customers' wants of the perceived benefits. In the private banking industry, a senior director gave this opinion:

> The pull-magnetism derived from a good reputation is the trickiest element of success in this business. There is no shop available for the client to shop around, even worse, the complexity of private banking services makes it very difficult for the client to evaluate service quality. Therefore a good reputation for a firm is the first contact with the client's mind, which constitutes a major force of pull magnetism.   (*Source*: anonymous)

Reputation, in such a case, serves as an important proxy for quality and assurance (Rumelt 1987).

Berry and Thompson (1982) suggested to the banking sector that the utility feature is a necessary condition for a further reciprocal relationship, and a long-term relationship can then be established. Crosby and Stephens (1987) found a significant path coefficient (.358), from satisfaction with a contact person to overall satisfaction. In view of the purpose of a relationship, the benefits of trust building are seen in the client's acquiescence, expectations for future relations, and of the preservation of the relation's retention. On the basis of sound reciprocity, various projecting efforts can then be facilitated, which may be categorised as: (1) cross-selling (Rose 1992, Surtani 1991); (2) maximising relationships in terms of cash flow (Howcroft and Whitehead 1990); (3) increasing costs of exit (Bharadwaj et al. 1993); (4) word of mouth publicity (File and Prince 1994); and (5) referral programs (Rose 1992). The more the company is able to achieve a closer bond with its customers, the more likely the projecting efforts will grow as essential means of relationship-building in the market place for marketers (Kotler 1991). Projecting strategies have been found to have a significant impact on business performance (Chien and Moutinho 1997). The associations among URLeP have been found to be interactive. These interactions describe levels of impact between the direction of legitimacy to utility, utility to reciprocity and reciprocity to projectability (Chien 1998, 1999). In other cases, the interaction of URLeP can be from utility to reciprocity; reciprocity to legitimacy, and legitimacy to projectability (Chien 2000).

Consistent results of the relationship model across different research phenomena provide compelling understanding. First, in the internal nature of an exchange relationship, utility, reciprocity, legitimacy and projectability (URLeP) are the dimensions to attract, maintain, and enhance a total relationship. The above explanation offers managers more specific strategic implications, instead of the 'all marketing activities' in Morgan and Hunt's (1994) definition of relationship marketing. Second, unlike the skewed focus of the antecedent-intermediate-consequence structure, there is no pre-defined role for any of the URLeP. They are naturally interactive in any form, which reflect consumer need for integrated communications or corporate efforts to adapt to their environment. Often, the way to categorise antecedence could leave an open-end redundancy that includes many possible factors without the theoretical scrutiny of a higher-level concept. Third, without a positive awareness of a legitimate image as a foundation for a pre-relationship, there is little chance for a company to overcome the threshold of prospects to enter into an exchange relation. Customers who do not acknowledge the other values of legitimacy, reciprocity and projectability, will act as opportunists. Such opportunistic relationships may be short-lived and eventually very costly. Therefore, it is suggested that companies should be alert when approaching a potential customer with utility value features without any pre-establishment of legitimacy. Fourth, without the pre-conditions of the positive awareness of a legitimate image and of satisfactory utility, efforts for reciprocal trust seem discourteous and burdensome.

Conclusion

What were we trying to achieve by presenting this multidimensional taxonomy of relationships? We wanted to explore the ambiguities surrounding achievement of utilitarian and other benefits. Within a framework of 'relationship', we determined to justify the argument of legitimacy and the accomplishment of fulfilment for parties involved in a [marketing] relationship. The concept of integrity was paramount here, as well as preservation of values. Despite uncertainty, the boundaries of relationship marketing, with all its related activities, interactivity and changing roles, should capitalise on the new directions reported here. Seeking to apply new dimensions of relationship marketing, and actual application, should lead to better customer retention and better business performance. As Levitt (1960) discovered years ago customer relationships really are the most important competitive assets.

References

Achrol, R. and Kotler, P. (1999) 'Marketing in the Network Economy', *Journal of Marketing*, Vol. 63, Special issue, pp. 146–163.

Anderson, E. and Barton, A.W. (1992) 'The Use of Pledges to Build and Sustain Commitment in Distribution Channels', *Journal of Marketing Research*, Vol. 29 No. 1 (February), pp. 18–34.

Anderson, J.C., and Narus, J.A. (1990) 'A Model of Distributor Firm and Manufacturer Firm Working Partnerships', *Journal of Marketing*, Vol. 54, No. 1 (January), pp. 42–58.

Bagozzi, R.P. (1979) 'Toward a Formal Theory of Marketing Exchange', in Ferrell, O., Brown, S. and Lamb, C. (eds) *Conceptual and Theoretical Developments in Marketing, American Marketing Association Proceedings*, pp. 431–447, New Jersey.

Bagozzi, R.P. (1995) 'Reflections on Relationship Marketing in Customer Markets', *Journal of the Academy of Marketing Science*, Vol. 23 No. 4 (Fall), pp. 272–277.

Baker, M. (1998), 'Relationship Marketing in Three Dimensions', *Journal of Interactive Marketing*, Vol. 8, No. 4 (Autumn), pp. 47–62.

Berry, L. (1995) 'Relationship Marketing of Services Growing Interest, Emerging Perspectives', *Journal of the Academy of Marketing Sciences*, Vol. 23, No. 4, pp. 236–245.

Berry, L.L. and Thompson, T. (1982), 'Relationship Banking: The Art of Turning Customers into Clients', *Journal of Retail Banking*, Vol. 4, No. 2, pp. 64–73.

Berscheid, E. and Peplau, L.A. (1983) The emerging science of close relationships. In H.H. Kelly, E. Berscheid, A. Christensen, J.H. Harvey, T.L. Huston, G. Levinger, E. McClintock, L.A. Peplau, and D.R. Peterson, *Close Relationship* (pp. 20–67), New York: Freeman.

Bharadwaj, S.G., Varadarajan, P. and Fahy, J. (1993) 'Sustainable Competitive Advantage in Service Industries: A Conceptual Model and Research Propositions', *Journal of Marketing*, Vol. 57, No. 4, (October), pp. 83–99.

Buss, D.M. and Kenrick, D.T. (1998) Evolutionary Social psychology. In D.T. Gilbert, S.T. Fiske and G. Lindzey (eds). *The handbook of social psychology* 4th ed., Vol. 2, pp. 982–1026. New York: McGraw-Hill.

Cacioppo, J.T., Berntson, G.G., Sheridan, J.F. and McClintock, M.K. (2000) 'Multilevel Integrative Analyses of Human Behavior: Social Neuroscience and the Complementing Nature of Social and Biological Approaches'. *Psychological Bulletin*, Vol. 126, No. 5, pp. 829–843.

Cannon, J.P. and Perreault Jr., W.D. (1999) 'Buyer-Seller Relationships in Business Markets', *Journal of Marketing Research*, Vol. 36, No. 4, (November), pp. 439–460.

Chien, S. and Moutinho, L. (1997) 'A Framework of Networking Effort – The Missing Part of Relationship Marketing', *Journal of Targeting Measurement & Analysis for Marketing*, Vol. 6, No. 1, pp. 12–20.

Chien, C.S. and Moutinho, L. (2000) 'The External Contingency and Internal Characteristic of Relationship Marketing', *Journal of Marketing Management*, Vol. 16, No. 4, pp. 583–595.

Courtesy L.L. Bean (1998) Company handout, Freeport, Maine.

Crosby, L.A. and Stephens, N. (1987) 'Effects of Relationship Marketing on Satisfaction, Retention, and Prices in the Life Insurance Industry', *Journal of Marketing Research*, Vol. 24 No. 4 (Nov.), pp. 404–411.

Day, G.S. (2000) 'Managing Market Relationships', *Journal of the Academy of Marketing Science*, Vol. 28. No. 1, pp. 24–30.

Day, G.S. and Montgomery, D.B. (1999) 'Charting New Directions for Marketing', *Journal of Marketing*, Vol. 63, Special Issues, pp. 3–13.

Doney, P.M. and Cannon, J.P. (1997) 'An Examination of the Nature of Trust in Buyer-Seller Relationships', *Journal of Marketing*, Vol. 61, No. 2 (April), 35–51.

Dwyer, F.R., Schurr, P.H. and Oh, S. (1987) 'Developing Buyer-Seller Relationships', *Journal of Marketing*, Vol. 51, No. 2 (April), pp. 11–27.

Fennel, M.L. and Alexander, J.A. (1987) 'Organisational Boundary Spanning in Institutionalised Environments', *Academy of Management Journal*, Vol. 30, No. 4, pp. 456–476.

File, K.M. and Prince, R.A. (1994) 'Marketing Offshore Private Banking', *International Journal of Bank Marketing*, Vol. 12, No. 3, pp. 4–8.

Fournier, S., Dobscha, S. and Mick, D. (1998) 'Preventing the Premature Death of Relationship Marketing', *Harvard Business Review*, Jan.–Feb., pp. 42–51.

Ganesan, S. (1994) 'Determinants of Long-Term Orientation in Buyer-Seller Relationships', *Journal of Marketing*, Vol. 58, (April), pp. 1–19.

Garbarino, E. and Johnson, M. (1999) 'The Different Roles of Satisfaction, Trust and Commitment for Relational and Transactional Consumers', *Journal of Marketing*, Vol. 63, No. 2 (April), pp. 70–87.

Grayson, K. and Ambler, T. (1999) 'The Dark Side of Long-term Relationships in Marketing Services', *Journal of Marketing Research*, Vol. 36, No. 1 (February), 132–141.

Gouldner, A.W. (1960) 'The Norm of Reciprocity: A Preliminary Statement', *American Sociological Review*, Vol. 25, No. 2, pp. 161–178.

Gruen, T.W., Summers, J.O. and Acito, F. (2000) 'Relationship Marketing Activities, Commitment, and Membership Behaviors in Professional Associations', *Journal of Marketing*, Vol. 64, No. 3 (July), 34–49.

Gummesson, E. (1999) *Total Relationship Marketing*, Oxford: Butterworth Heinemann.

Hirsch, P. (1975) 'Organisational Effectiveness and the Institutional Environment', *Administrative Science Quarterly*, Vol. 20, No. 3, pp. 327–344.

Howcroft, J.B. and Whitehead, M. (1990) 'The Single European Market: The Challenge to Commercial Banking', *International Journal of Bank Marketing*, Vol. 8, No. 1, pp. 12–18.

Hunt, Shelby D. (1991) *Modern Marketing theory*. Cincinnati, OH: South-Western Publishing Co.

Kelley, H. and Thibaut, J.W. (1978) *Interpersonal Relations: A Theory of Interdependence*, John Wiley and Sons, New York.

Lemon, K., White, B. and Winer, R. (2002) 'Dynamic Customer Relationship Management: Incorporating Future Considerations into the Service Retention Decision', *Journal of Marketing*, Vol. 66, No. 1 (January), pp. 1–14.

Levitt, T. (1960) 'Marketing Myopia' *Harvard Business Review*, July–August.

Macneil, I.R. (1980) *The New Social Contract: An Inquiry into Modern Contractual Relations*. New Heaven, CT: Yale University Press.

Mahajan, V., Srinivasan, R. and Wind, J. (2002) 'The Dot.com Retail Failures of 2000: Were There Any Winners?' *Journal of the Academy of Marketing Science*, Vol. 30, No. 4, pp. 474–486.

Meyer, J.W. and Scott, W.R. (1983) *Organisational Environments: Ritual and Rationality*, Sage, Beverly Hills, CA.

Moorman, C., Zaltman, G. and Deshpande, R. (1992) 'Relationships Between Providers and Users of Market Research: The Dynamic of Trust Within and between Organisations', *Journal of Marketing Research*, Vol. 29, No. 3 (August), 314–328.

Morgan, R.M. and Hunt, S.D. (1994) 'The Commitment-Trust Theory of relationship marketing', *Journal of Marketing*, Vol. 58, No. 1 (July), 20–38.

Oliver, C. (1990) 'Determinants of Interorganisational Relationships: Integration and Future Directions', *Academy of Management Review*, Vol. 15, No. 2, pp. 241–265.

Palmer, A. (2002) 'The Evolution of an Idea: An Environmental Explanation of Relationship Marketing', *Journal of Relationship Marketing*, Vol. 1, No. 1, pp. 79–94.

Peppers, D. and Rogers, M. (1993) *The One to One Future*, New York: Doubleday.

Peppers, D. and Rogers, M. (1997) *Enterprise One to One Future*, New York: Doubleday.

Reinartz, W.J. and Kumar, V. (2000) 'On the Profitability of Long-Life Customers in a Noncontractual Setting: An Empirical Investigation and Implications for marketing', *Journal of Marketing*, Vol. 64, No. 4 (October), 17–35.

Reis, H.T., Collins W.A. and Berscheid E. (2000) 'The Relationship Context of Human behavior and Development', *Psychological Bulletin*, Vol. 126, No. 6, 844–872.

Rose, S. (1992) 'A New Approach To Private Banking', *Journal of Retail Banking*, Vol. 14, No. 2, pp. 11–15.

Rumelt, R.P. (1987) 'Theory, Strategy and Entrepreneurship', in *The Competitive Challenge: Strategies for Industrial Innovation and Renewal*, Ballinger Publishing Co., Cambridge MA.

Sheth, J.N. and Parvatiyar, A. (2002) 'Evolving Relationship Marketing into a Discipline', *Journal of Relationship Marketing*, Vol. 1, No.1, pp. 3–16.

Siew, M.L. (1985) 'Metatheory and Metamethodology in Marketing: A Lakatosian Reconstruction', *Journal of Marketing*, Vol. 49, No. 4 (Fall), pp. 23–40.

Taylor, S., Pham, L., Rivkin, I. and Armor, D. (1998) 'Harnessing the Imagination: Mental Simulation, Self-regulation and Coping', *American Psychologist*, Vol. 53, No. 4, pp. 429–439.

Taylor, S. and Pham, L. (1996) 'Mental Simulations, Motivation and Action', in *The Psychology of Action: Linking Cognition and Motivation to Behavior*, in P. Gollwitzer, Bargh, J. (eds), New York: Guilford Press, pp. 219–235.

Teas, R.K. and Palan, K.M. (1997) 'The Realms of Scientific Meaning Framework for Constructing Theoretically Meaningful Nominal Definitions of Marketing Concepts', *Journal of Marketing*, Vol. 61, No. 2 (April), pp. 52–67.

Webster, F.E. (1992) 'The Changing Role of Marketing in the Corporation', *Journal of Marketing*, Vol. 56, No. 4 (October), pp. 1–17.

Williamson, O.E. (1985) *The Economic Institutions of Capitalism: Firms, Markets, Relational Contracting*, Free Press, New York.

Wilson, D.T. (1995) 'An Integrated Model of Buyer-Seller Relationships', *Journal of the Academy of Marketing Science*, Vol. 23. No. 4 (Fall), pp. 335–345.

Zucker, L.G. (1986) 'Production of trust: Institutional sources of economic structure 1840–1920', In *Research in Organisation Behavior*, B.M. Staw and L.L Cummings (eds), Vol. 8, pp. 53–111, Greenwich, CT: JAI Press.

Notes

Chapter 5 Invisible Forces: How Consumer Interactions Make the Difference

1. In this case auto-catalytically proliferating means a (sexual) reproduction that leads to population growth without any external influence.
2. ICQ is about creating simple, massively popular ways to communicate online. ICQ was a first internet-wide instant messenger launched in 1996. Today, with over 150 million registered users, ICQ is one of the largest and most active global communities.

Chapter 8 Beyond Relationship Marketing

1. Formal language systems are different from natural languages. Unlike having the vague and continually evolving formation rules of natural languages, such as English, formal language systems identify all of the primitive elements and rigorously specify the formation rules delineating the permissible logic to combine the primitive elements to form conceptual statements (Hunt 1991).
2. Primitive terms are undefined basic elements of the formal language system, like the building stones of theories (Bunge 1967). Derived terms, in contrast, are derived from the primitive elements (Hunt 1991).
3. Relationship is seen as a governance mechanism in relational exchange, and trust and commitment are key attributes of relationship (Anderson and Narus 1990; Heide and John 1992, Morgan and Hunt 1994). Also, an alternative view of relationship has emerged a network perspective of relationship that emphases the relating mechanism between exchange partners (Achrol and Kotler 1999, Day 2000, Deshpande 1999).

Index

3M, 127

academics, 30–31
Academy of Marketing Debate, 30
accountability, lack of, 14
accounting value, 19
adaptive complex system, 62
adoption curve, 60, 61, 62, 66
advertisements, 67, 68, 99, 102, 103, 106
Agency Partnership Process, 119
agency-client partnership, 100
alliances, 77, 83, 86
Amazon, 97
American Marketing Association (AMA), 3
anecdotal evidence, 63, 73
anti-globalisation, 83
AOL, 97
'archeological' knowledge, 73
Artificial Intelligence, 74
attitudinal directions, 122
Automobile Association, 97

banking sector, 138
Bass diffusion pattern, 64
Bass, Frank, 60, 64
benefits and burdens, 125, 132
best practice, 97, 98
   firms, 46
   studies, 38
blue-chip companies, 6, 14
Bluetooth-enabled, 82
Brand-Customer Community Research, 119
BrandPrint, 117
brand(s), 79, 80, 83, 85, 86, 91
   -acutalisation, 104
   assets, 35
   awareness, **27**
   development, 16
   equity, 20, 138
   experience, 98, 99, 108

meaning, 107
name, 68, 82
power of, 16
preference, **27**
success, 19
valuation, 37
Brand-Customer Community Research, 119
Bridgestone, 81
Britain's top companies, 21, **22**
British Gas, 105, 110
business process re-engineering (BPR), 15, 28, 101
buyer-seller relationship, 123

Calvino, I., 8, 9
case studies, 1, 90–95, 118
   Coca-Cola, 90–2
   Volkswagen, 93–95
case study analysis, 60
Cellular Automata, 62, 66, 67
Centre for Integrated Marketing, 98, 101, 117
Centrica, 98, 118
CEOs, 15, 29, 30, 98
Chartered Institute of Marketing (CIM), x, xi, 3, 32, 98
choice-induced exchange, 137
commitment, 128, 129, 136, 137
company value, 18
competition, 43–57
   efficiency, 44, 45, 46
   flexibility, 44, 45, 47
   long-term, 47
   marginal differentiation, 44, 45
   proprietariness, 44, 45, 46, 47
   square of, 44
   triangle of, 43
   zero-sum, 44
competitive
   advantage, 5
   assets, 140
   edge, 21

144